Legal Disclaimer

This book highlights different ways to find and recruit diverse candidates for your job openings online. Please consult your Country's HR compliance in regards to Diversity recruiting. This includes understanding GDPR and OFCCP employment compliance. Discretion is advised before doing any of the suggestions listed in this book.

Table of Contents

A Guide to Diversity Talent Sourcing

By: Jonathan Kidder

"Jonathan Kidder is well known to many of us in the Recruiting industry as the WizardSourcer - so it's hardly surprising that he has written the definitive Guide to Diversity Recruiting. From Search Modifiers to Talent Mapping, from Boolean strings to Sourcing tools - Jonathan pretty much leaves no stone unturned in his successful quest to deliver a roadmap for Recruiters, to truly own the art and science of Diversity Recruiting in 2021 and beyond. Excellent!" --Marcus Edwardes, Recruiting Trail Blazers Podcast

"This guide is an awesome reference for anyone who wants to be doing better with their Diversity Sourcing and Recruiting. But it is more than that. It is also a good reminder to be more creative when it comes to finding talent in general. I highly recommend this read for anyone who wants to improve their Sourcing Skills. Thanks for sharing your wealth of knowledge so freely and succinctly, Jonathan!" --Vanessa Raath, Founder of the Talent Hunter

"A practical guide, finally! The Diversity & Inclusion is an enormous topic on the minds of CEOs of many companies but how to get started on the D&I strategy is often a question. Inevitably it is about listening and understanding your own employees first and creating an inclusive culture within your company. Then it is about sourcing and hiring diverse talent. Jonathan's book is finally coming with practical tips, advice and guidance that many Talent Acquisition teams were waiting for. This book is a must-read for all modern recruiters and sourcers." --Josef Kadlec, Trainer, Speaker, Author, and Founding CEO of Recruitment Academy

A Guide to Diversity Talent Sourcing

How to attract and hire diverse candidates using Boolean strings and tools online. Use this book as a guide to understand how to find diverse talent available online. The Book will highlight Boolean String examples and suggest different Talent Sourcing tools to use when you create a Diversity Talent Sourcing strategy. The goal of the book is to give you resources and tools to create a strategy when it comes to D&I recruiting goals within your company.

The author of this book has almost over a decade of research talent sourcing experience. Jonathan Kidder has trained Sourcers across the globe and he's an active blogger within the community. He launched his blog WizardSourcer.com in 2015 which focuses on helping others learn about the latest talent sourcing tools.

He's excited to share the latest diversity Boolean strings and recruitment tools on the market and, even more so, he's excited to help you on your journey of becoming a Wizard at talent sourcing.

Once this book was published in 2021, the string and tool suggestions were already out of date. Technology moves fast within the recruiting space. There will always be a newer and better tool out in the market. I wanted to highlight tools that have been tried and true for a while within the D&I space.

About Jonathan Kidder

Jonathan Kidder, AKA the "WizardSourcer," is a top-ranked technical talent sourcing recruiter, staffing expert, and corporate trainer who assists organizations of all sizes in identifying and attracting top talent.

A wizard at harnessing the power of social networking, Boolean strings, search aggregators, deep web searching, scrapers, and other advanced technology tricks and tools. In 2015, he founded a recruiting blog called WizardSourcer, which has become one of the leading knowledge resources for recruiters online.

His mission is simple: To help Recruiters and Sourcers effectively launch a Diversity Talent Sourcing plan at their company.

With nearly a decade of full-cycle recruiting and sourcing experience under his belt, he has worked in talent sourcing and recruiting with companies including Amazon, Vista Outdoor, CA Technologies, American Express, and many others.

Throughout his career as a sourcing leader, he has pursued continuous learning to stay current on the latest sourcing trends and to help clients across industries maximize the use of high-tech recruiting tools ranging from browser extensions to AI automation.

After earning a bachelor's in business from Bethel University in Saint Paul, Minnesota, Jonathan launched his sourcing career at Allegis Global Solutions, one of the largest RPO staffing companies in the world.

At Allegis, Jonathan discovered the power of social media as a recruiting tool. This inspired him to develop and implement a proprietary employer branding EVP and recruitment marketing plan that could be used with any client to attract the world's best available talent.

A sought-after speaker and mentor, Jonathan has trained teams around the globe on best practices for sourcing and recruiting top talent. One of the industry's emerging go-to resources on recruiting expertise in the 21st century, he writes regularly on the latest recruiting trends for his own top-ranked blog at WizardSourcer in addition to being a contributing writer for AI recruiting platform Hiretual and Recruitingblogs.com.

He is the author of LinkedIn Revealed and Top Talent Sourcing Tools books. He currently lives in Minneapolis with his wife and adopted golden doodle dog named Henry.

If you purchased a paperback copy but would like a digital PDF version to easily copy Boolean strings within a search please reach out to me on my website here: WizardSourcer.com/contact

Chapter 1: Defining Diversity

The concept of diversity encompasses acceptance and respect. It means understanding that each individual is unique and recognizing our individual differences. These can be along the dimensions of race, ethnicity, gender, sexual orientation, socio-economic status, age, physical abilities, religious beliefs, political beliefs, or other ideologies.

In regards to Diversity and Inclusion within the recruiting space, this includes attracting talent from a diverse applicant pool. A diverse plan is defined as (BLNA) which means Black, Latin, or Native American.

Some Statistics on Diversity Recruiting:

67% of active and passive job seekers say diversity is important to them when they're evaluating companies and job offers. (Glassdoor)

32% of job seekers ranked diversity as "important," and 18% as "not important."
(Jobvite)

96% of job seekers say that it's important to work for a company that embraces transparency. (Glassdoor)

80% of job seekers believe their companies foster diversity at work. (Jobvite)

37% of recruiters ranked recruiting more diverse candidates as a top trend in the near future.
(LinkedIn)

Gender diverse companies are 15% more likely to have a financial performance above the industry mean. (McKinsey)

There are only 4 African American CEOs (all men) of Fortune 500 companies, accounting for 2% of the list. (Fortune 500)

These statistics are quite shocking. That's why I wanted to write about this topic-- to showcase Boolean strings and talent sourcing tools that will help guide Recruiters to find great diverse candidates online.

Here's a general guide to follow when you are trying to connect with diverse leads online:

1. Do not use the typical outreach method at the beginning. Instead, be more empathic and transparent.

2. Understand the purpose behind the community. Whether it's a group or non-profit try to understand the mission.

3. Reach out to leader of group, association, or non-profit and let them know your purpose.

4. Focus on building long term relationships with local leaders.

5. Put yourself in their shoes and recognize that this is a safe space for that particular group.

6. Be mindful that you're representing your company's brand when interacting with passive leads.

Chapter 2: How to Search for Diverse Candidates

Understanding search modifiers & operators fundamentals

Searching is a major part of any recruiter's job, and luckily, Google makes it quite easy to find what you're looking for, so long as you go beyond the basic word search option. Once you learn Google's advanced search operators, you can find exactly what you need in far less time. The key is knowing which to use and when. Here's a look at the top Google Search Operators that recruiters can use when sourcing for diverse candidates. Make sure to review all of these examples as. you will be able to use them later on within the book.

site:example.com

This is one of the most basic search operators you can use, and it will certainly come in handy. This will produce two pieces of information: the list of pages in the site's index and the number of pages in the site's index.

site:example.com/folder

Want to dive deeper into a site's sub-folder, like "/blog"? This is the search operator to use. Add it to the end of any root domain and you'll soon have all the info you need.

site:sub.example.com

If you want to get down into a site's sub-domains, this search operator is another good one to use.

site:example.com inurl:www

This operator can help you find a domain's sub-domain.

Add a [-] to exclude options

If you add a "-" before the search operator of number four, you'll be able to tell Google to find anything except that specific text. In this case, you can use it in front of "inurl:www" to find any indexed URLs for that site that don't have the "www" sub-domain, as in: site:example.com -inurl:www.

Chain operators to get more done

Most operators can be chained, which means you can get to very specific information just by combining different operators to produce the search you want to perform.

For example: site:example.com -inurl:www -inurl:dev -inurl:shop.

site:example.com inurl:https

If you want to find any secure pages on a site, you can use this operator.

site:example.com inurl:param

If you're worried about pagination, search sorts, or something else, using "inurl" and a parameter to track down pages is handy.

site:example.com -inurl:param

This operator allows you to know all sorts of things, like how many pages are being indexed for a specific website without sorts.

site:example.com text goes here

You can also combine the "site" operator with a plain text query. This means you'll be able to search a page's entire content for certain or relevant text. Google will try to match all the terms you put in, but they may be separated or the search may only return certain terms.

site:example.com "text goes here"

If you want an exact match to the text you put in, simply surround your text with quotation marks and Google will look for an exact match. This is great for tracking down specific details.

site:example.com/folder "text goes here"

You can also use the above operator to check for content within a specific folder, whether you're looking for an exact match (with quotations) or just any relevant results (without quotations).

site:example.com this OR that

Google does allow you to use "OR" in your queries if you are looking for something specific. If you don't know what exact term you're looking for out of a couple options, this operator could be very useful.

site:example.com "top * ways"

The asterisk acts as a wildcard, allowing you to look for unknown text.

site:example.com "top 7..10 ways"

If you have a number range in mind for a search, you can always search using X...Y. It will return anything within the range of X to Y.

Pro tip: you can search graduations dates or years of experience using this operator function i.e. > 2009..2011

site:example.comintitle:"text goes here"

When you search for something using the "intitle" operator, it will only return text that's within <TITLE> tags.

site:example.com intitle:"text * here"

You can vary the last few operators to use "intitle:"

intitle:"text goes here"

This "intitle" search returns matching queries from across the entire web.

"text goes here" -site:example.com

This operator allows you to find text on any site while excluding a certain domain. It could be useful if you're trying to find a company or candidate's info outside of their main website or profile.

site:example.com filetype:pdf

If you're looking for something of a specific file type, using the "filetype" search operator is the way to go. For instance, this one allows you to find all PDFs on a given domain, but you can search for other formats, too.

I've included a guide for modifiers and operators below:

"Search Keyword"	Exact match search
OR	Search for X or Y
AND (Space)	Search for X and Y

*	Wildcards will match any word or phrase
( )	Multiple terms
(-)	Minus excludes keywords or phrases
define:	Dictionary search feature
cache:	Most recent cache version of a website page
filetype:	Searching for file types i.e. PDF, DOCX, TXT, PPT, or CSV
site:	Xraying one entire website
related:	Find sites related to a given domain

info:	Shows page info
intitle:	Find a certain word (or words) in the title
allintitle:	Only results containing all of the specified words in the title tag will be returned
inurl:	Find pages with a certain word (or words) in the URL
allinurl:	Only results containing all of the specified words in the URL will be returned
intext:	Find pages containing a certain word (or words)
allintext:	Only results containing all of the specific words on a page

AROUND(X)	Proximity search. Find pages containing two words or phrases within X words of each other
source:	Finding a news related source on Google
#..#	Search for a range of numbers
inanchor:	Find pages that are being linked to with specific anchor text
allinanchor:	Only results containing all of the specified words in the inbound anchor text

Source: https://wizardsourcer.com/boolean-strings-list

How do Search Engines work?
Search engines work by crawling hundreds of billions of pages using their own web crawlers. These web crawlers are commonly referred to as search engine bots or spiders. A search engine navigates the web by downloading web pages and following links on these pages to discover new pages that have been made available.

Search Engines that I recommend using:

- Google
- Bing
- DuckDuckgo
- Yippy
- Uvrx

Where can I find people online?
While not every candidate promotes his or her diversity online, searches for "natural language" phrases (for example: "Spanish speaking") relating to ethnicities and languages can be useful when sourcing. You can also search for diverse fraternities or sororities, universities, and professional associations.

To find the candidates you want, you have to be able to understand the phrases used online when they describe themselves.

Using phrasing that contains pronouns and action words ("I configured *" OR "I presented at *) will point you in the direction of relevant resumes and social media profiles as well.

You will need to expand on how you were taught to conduct a search on a search engine. In order to find diverse talent, you will need to search social networks, communities, and groups that they might associate with instead of including a race or gender keyword within your search.

How to Create a Diversity Sourcing Strategy
A company recruiting team will first need to create a D&I plan. Once you've set goals for hiring, the next step is to create a talent sourcing strategy.

If you are striving to hire a more diversified staff, you're probably thinking about how you can update your recruiting strategies to help better attract diverse applicants. The fact is, in order to reach a fair amount of underrepresented minority candidates, you need to recruit in a purposeful and focused manner.

You just can't wait for qualified and BLNA leads to apply for your roles. You'll need to have your Sourcing team focus on building a strategy. Below is how to build a diversity sourcing strategy at your company.

Tips for Diverse Recruiting
These tips aren't perfect, but with some trial-and-error, you'll be able to implement them into your practices and get better results.

Launch Objectives and Milestones: As once said, "A dream without a plan is just a wish," and what's a plan without goals? You should start by determining the milestones you need to hit to consider your changes successful overtime. Track all your metrics and create a sourcing goal for each week, month, and quarter.

Get Creative with Platforms: Out with the old, in with the new. While some traditional methods still work great, others are quickly becoming outdated and they're leaving out a lot of diverse talent.

Experiment with Engagement: Those outreach templates you've been using might just need to be revamped to reflect more welcoming, universal language and to make them more appealing to the modern worker in general. Ask for Referrals – use your diverse employees and have them better represent your employment brand. Get them involved in your outreach efforts.

Creating a Diversity Sourcing Power Hour:
This is honestly my one number suggestion in this book!

Have your team dedicate 1-3 hours a week to sourcing diverse leads. Send a weekly calendar invite to block off the needed time. During this hour you can either allow the team to quietly source and search for leads or you can invite speakers to present on diversity sourcing tips/tricks. Create a fun and lively event that highlights your Sourcers abilities. Share weekly success stories and discuss obstacles that are team is currently facing.

During the power hour sessions, make sure to create a live excel document to track all your teams recruiting efforts. Showcase this data to managers and present it to your leadership team.

Here's how we track our current leads in my process:

Pro tip: Try cold calling candidates after standard work hours. Some candidates may have different work schedules outside of a 9-5 pm type of role.

Find More Diverse Talent
Get started with this advice today and begin recruiting a more diverse workforce to your open positions. While it takes time and dedication to seek out leads in the underrepresented segments of the population, it's an endeavor that will prove well worth it. Start by tracking your recruiting metrics!

How to Build a Diversity Talent Pipeline

Creating a talent pipeline of diverse leads will take time.

Companies are seeing the value of having a diverse employee workforce. Every company wants to attract and retain the most qualified applicants and finding applicants with a diverse

19

background can be very challenging. I've had my own difficulties trying to source for diverse talent.

Here's how to create a diversity talent pipeline to fill your roles:

It's taken me several years to understand the market and to come up with a strategy that worked for me. You can waste a lot of time in the wrong places. I don't recommend going to job fairs or outplacement firms I have never had success with using these types of resources. However, here are some ideas that do work to recruit and source diverse leads.

1. Facebook Job Ads

These ads can be a cost-effective way to target certain demographics. Videos are popular on social media and it helps if you can include a job description with a video ad. This would be the best way to target diverse applicants in a certain location. For less than $500, you would have a creative advertisement that draws in views and traffic. You can also use Boolean strings to directly source on Facebook. It's really an untapped market for talent.

Once your ad is active – you can share the post within diverse / niche groups on Facebook! There's so many active community groups that are focused on BLNA networks.

Facebook has roughly a billon active users every month. That's why it's a great place to post a job that your company might have. A Recruiter primarily focuses on the standard job boards like Indeed, CareerBuilder, and LinkedIn but it's good to think outside these standards.

You need to get more creative and go where your niche pays attention to. If you are targeting GenX or Millennials than Facebook would be a great alternative instead of regular job board. Diverse (BLNA) leads, Blue-collar, and other industries that probably don't have a professional LinkedIn profile probably have a Facebook profile.

Benefits of posting a job on Facebook include reaching a vast applicant pool that might not visit other websites online. This is also a great avenue if you are on a shoe string budget. Facebook Ads for job postings are free within the platform. If your company has a great employment brand within social media than why not benefit from this and post a job on Facebook?

Here's How to Post a Job on Facebook:

Use your companies Facebook Company page if you are an independent or boutique firm, then use your Staffing firms corporate page.

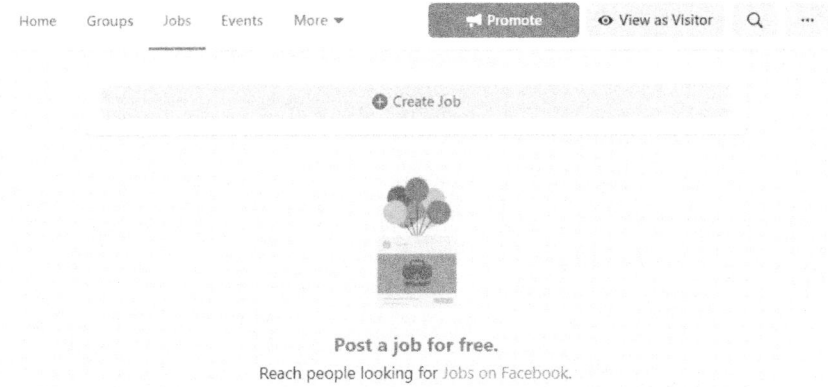

Create the job advertisement for free and click publish:

Information Includes:

- Job title
- Job Location
- Job Type
- Salary Range
- Add Additional Question
- Receive applications by email
- Require Resume Upload
- Include an image

Showcase an Image

Ads with images are more clicked and viewed within Facebook. I recommend adding a company logo or a professional picture of your team or organization. Below is a basic measurement for images sizes within Facebook:

- Post: 940 x 788
- In-feed ad image: 1200 x 628
- Right column ad image: 1200 x 628
- Carousel ad image: 600 x 600

Showcase a Video Ad

You can also include a video description within an ad. You can use this to showcase your team and employment brand. Get creative with your ads and generate some solid engagement.

Easily Manage Job Applicants

Within the setting bar, you can view your applicants and manage your published job ads.

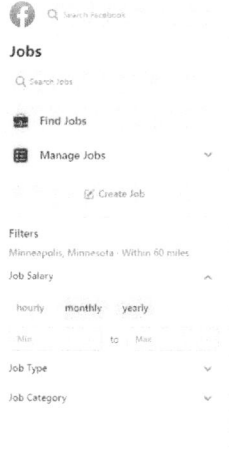

Here's Tips from Facebook on Attracting Job Applicants:

- Describe the job thoroughly
- Provide key details
- Fill in the specifics
- Use additional questions
- Stay organized

- Respond promptly

Target Communities Online:

1. Colleges & Universities

Target a variety of schools with diverse populations. I've had success by just googling different schools and their diversity outreach programs. You can even email the career service department. Usually, career services are more than willing to post your job and broadcast your opportunity on email chains or alumni websites. You can also ask about opportunities to set up a table at any future events they might be having.

2. Non-profits & Associations

Do some research on non-profits and associations in your target location. These organizations have many community-building events. They have a strong network that could really help with a tough search. I would recommend having them post your opportunity and see what other ways they can partner with you in finding qualified candidates.

3. Religious Institutions

I've had some success by contacting different churches and religious organizations. They usually have event calendars listed on their websites. This is a great way to find community based events.

3. Networking for Referrals

Always ask your employees for referrals. Usually the hiring manager has strong ties with the local market. They may have colleges and events in their network that they already know of. You can even have an applicant with a diverse background write a testimonial of their experience at the company. This could help with building a culture that supports and attracts top diverse applicants.

Overall, it takes a lot of effort to build a diverse pipeline. I've had a lot of success with attracting diverse applicants, but there are always ways in which I can improve my strategies. I recommend writing down all your ideas and creating time-bound goals. What are some of the creative ways that you engage diverse talent?

How to Create a Team Sourcing Jam Session
Use your company's internal teams to source for referrals. Create a talent sourcing jam event and encourage them to reach out to their own personal networks online.

Some people might say we're all truly connected to each other and in some ways, life is a small world. I've been fortunate enough to have had a long career in the talent sourcing space. If you would ask me if I knew any Talent Sourcers who might be a good fit for a role I could name off more than a dozen prospects.

Maybe you've heard of the Kevin Bacon effect? If you sat down with friends and chose an actor or actress odds are after 4-5 names that individual played a role with Kevin Bacon. You can use this same concept when bringing a team of professionals together and having them source through their own networks.

Say you're looking for an FP&A Manager? – The team that you have at your company has many diverse backgrounds. They probably have a network of leads that you can certainly tap into – especially in a tight job market. The idea to crowd-source for leads has been around for many years and this practice is called a "Sourcing Jam."

A Talent Sourcing Jam involves inviting a team together and having them go through their network for possible candidate leads. You can also use their expertise to help target passive leads on social media sites like LinkedIn or many others.

How to set up a Talent Sourcing Jam Session:

1. Use the data to figure on which roles have been a challenge for your company.

2. Invite hiring managers and other leaders within that department.

3. Try and have at least 3-6 members attend the event.

4. If you have a budget, I recommend bringing snacks. Make it become a fun and engaging event.

5. Setting expectations over email:

- State the reasoning behind the email.
- Have them bring their laptops and LinkedIn account login.
- If they've attended conferences or associations – have them bring an attendees list.

6. Come the event day be prepared to write suggestions on a white board. It's also nice to have someone write down those board suggestions in google docs and share that live document with the whole team.

7. Whether you're focusing on skill-sets, job titles, companies, or universities to target, use those areas to map out a network of referral suggestions. You can set a timer down and have them search through their network. Write down every suggestion on that white board.

8. Depending on privacy issues once you have the list created, you can have the Talent Sourcers reach out to the lead suggestions or have those individuals reach out directly.

9. Turn this event into bi-monthly or quarterly event. Get them excited by turning it into a game. Have prizes or incentives for

hires. Food and prizes are a great way to bring everyone together.

For example, my manager treated the event almost like a Jeopardy game. He plays music and acts like Alex Trebek when going through people's networks and we had a blast.

Here's an Email Template that you can send your Hiring Manager:

Hi (Name) – we have a lot of sourcing needs for this team and would like to have a sourcing lunch session.

Team Objective:

Spend an hour finding referrals & leads to reach out to for our openings.

Food will be provided. (Please give me suggestions).

During this hour, we will have each of your login into LinkedIn and search for potential leads and add them into a google doc.

After the meeting, me and Rachel would reach out to those leads and start them in our process.

Please let us know if you have any further questions!

Overall, there's a HUGE benefit to bringing a team together to help them source within their own networks. On top of that, it also helps improve your relationships with the talent acquisition teams and helps the Talent Sourcer(s) refocus and target on the right leads for job openings.

How to Create a Recruitment Tracker Template
I would recommend creating a recruitment tracker to track all your diversity sourcing efforts.

A lot of work goes into the recruiting process and it's important to stay organized during every step. The full cycle process includes: sourcing, screening, submitting, and setting up final round interviews. Every part involves various steps and procedures depending on your organization. You will need to coordinate with recruiting coordinators, internal teams, and applicants throughout the entire process. Having a well-organized Recruitment Tracker template that is simple and easy to understand will be important. I recommend creating a basic template within Microsoft Excel, Google Sheets, Trello, or Airtable.

Below are Step-by-Step Instructions on Creating a Recruitment Tracker Template:

Date	Role	Location	Full Name	Email	Cell	Salary	BLNA	Interview 1	Onsite Ready	Final Round

- Date: Include the date when you first sourced the candidate lead.
- Role: Include the role and req number that you are sourcing for.
- Location: Include the State or City where the candidate is based.
- Full Name: Include the full name of the candidate.
- Contact Information: Include the candidate's personal email address and cell number.
- Salary Expectation: Once you screen the candidate, get their all-in salary expectations. Include additional details like bonus and stock plans.
- BLNA: If the candidate self-selects there (race) and it's diverse (BLNA) you can track this as well.

- Phone Screen: Once you review applicants and sourced leads the next steps will be to schedule a phone screen call.
- Interview OR Assessment: Within this column, you can get the candidates interviewing availability for the first round interview or online assessment.
- Candidates Onsite Ready: If the candidates pass the first round, the next steps will be to schedule a final round interview.
- Final Round (Hired): Once the final round happens, the team will then decide to either decline or move forward with an offer.

Use Colors to Highlight each Step in your process

- Gray: Separate each sourcing week with the document.
- Green: Highlight candidates who are onsite ready.
- Yellow: Candidate who have withdrawn from the process.
- Orange: Candidates interested in the future and require a follow up.

Weekly Recap Tracker Template

In another tab create a weekly recap of your sourcing metrics. This is a great way to showcase data to your manager or hiring manager.

Funnel Tracker				
Per Week	Outreach	Phone Screens	1 Round	On-Site Ready
April 8th	108	10	9	2
April 15th	55	8	8	1
April 22nd	125	8	7	2
April 29th	89	10	10	1
May 6th	112	8	6	1
May 13th	50	10	10	1
May 20th	75	7	6	1
May 27th	70	8	6	2
June 3rd	129	8	8	1
June 10th	115	7	6	2
June 17th	51	9	0	0

Offer Accepts Tracker Template

Use this template to track all of your offer accept hires for the year.

Offer Accepts	Hires	Level	BLNA
1			
2			
3			
4			
5			
6			
7			
8			
9			
10			

Chapter 3: Creating a Diversity Talent Mapping Plan

Talent mapping is defined as researching your company's competition in relation to job openings and then using that data when you start to source candidates. You can also present this data to your hiring manager to help them understand the level of difficulty and challenge that you might face in finding candidates in certain locations.

Talent Mapping Tools:
These tools will help you monitor, track, and find leads online.

Owler - With this tool, you can create custom company lists and receive news about these specific companies through the web or email.

Company Profiles
Access crucial company data, including annual revenue, employee count, location, funding history, acquisitions, recent news, and more.

Meet the world's most up-to-date competitive graph in existence! Owler maps over 40 million competitive relationships between 13 million companies worldwide.

Advanced Search
Filter Owler's entire company database by annual revenue, sector, location, employee count, and public/private company status.

RANK	COMPANY	CEO		CEO RATING	EMPLOYEES	FUNDING	REVENUE
	wealthfront		Andy Rachleff President & CEO	80/100	181	$204.7M	$29M
1	**Betterment**		Jonathan Stein Co-Founder & CEO	84/100	320	$275M	$30M
2	acorns		Noah Kerner CEO	81/100	390	$255.6M	$8.7M
3	personal CAPITAL		Jay Shah President & CEO	86/100	800	$314.3M	$22.4M
4	Robinhood		Baiju Prafulkumar Bhatt Co-CEO	84/100	1,281	$1.7B	$60M

See 83 more competitors

Glassdoor - Can give you a valuable point of view of a company's employees. Track your competition and gain Intel on local markets.

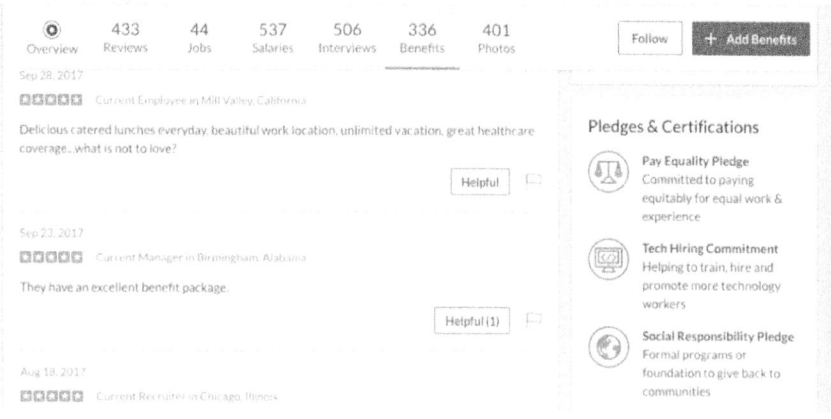

Justice Maps - Use this data to understand where diverse candidates may live across North America:

Source: http://www.justicemap.org

What data layers do you have?

We have several race layers and income layers (three different representations of median household income). The race layers are available at the county, census tract, block group, and block level. The income layers are available at the county and census tract level. This provides greater detail when you zoom in.

Zipwho.com - This ZIP code demographics site was built because existing census statistics tools failed to satisfy the needs of power users. Many Web sites allow users to query the median household income of a ZIP code, but that dollar figure alone does not indicate how one neighborhood's population compares to others around the country. ZipWho.com fills this information gap by displaying a national percentile rank (0 - 99) next to every data element.

Basic ZIP Code Search

ZIP Code 55422
Basic Search

Advanced Demographics Search

State: Minnesota ▾   Advanced Search

City: Golden Valley   (optional)

[Choose Demographic Attribute] ▾
between [ ] and [ ]

[Choose Demographic Attribute] ▾
between [ ] and [ ]

[Choose Demographic Attribute] ▾
between [ ] and [ ]

[Choose Demographic Attribute] ▾
between [ ] and [ ]

55422: Minneapolis, MN

		National Percentile Rank (0-99)
Median Income ($)	51,885	78
Cost Of Living Index	133.9	68
Median Mortgage To Income Ratio (%)	19.7	29
Owner Occupied Homes (%)	77.1	50
Median Rooms In Home	5.8	69
College Degree (%)	33.8	84
Professional (%)	41.5	85
Population	27,970	84
Average Household Size	2.3	15
Median Age	39.3	73
Male To Female Ratio (%)	90.2	39
Married (%)	54.6	21
Divorced (%)	10.3	63
White (%)	87.9	47
Black (%)	5.3	68
Asian (%)	2.1	79
Hispanic Ethnicity (%)	2.0	51

City-Data.com - By collecting and analyzing data from a variety of government and private sources, was able to create detailed, informative profiles for every city in the United States. From race demographics, crime rates, to weather patterns, you'll find the data you're looking for on City-Data.com.

Minnesota Bigger Cities (over 6000 residents)

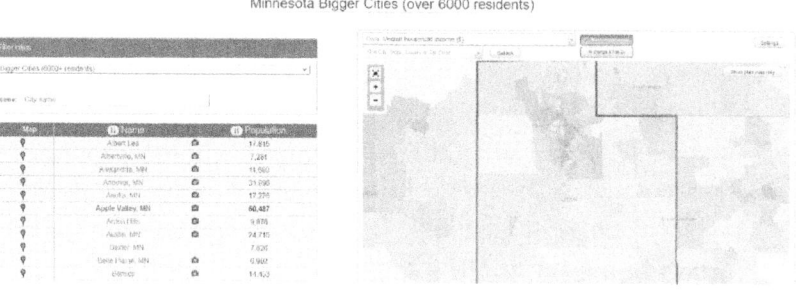

Where to Source Diversity Leads in North America:

It takes research to understand where diverse candidates may live. There's a lot of great resources online - primarily I recommend checking out Wikipedia.

Top 10 Cities with highest % of Black or African-Americans

City	Total population	(Black or African-American)	
		Rank	Percentage of total population
Detroit, Michigan	713,777	1	84.3
Jackson, Mississippi	173,514	2	80.1
Miami Gardens,	107,167	3	77.9

Florida			
Birmingham, Alabama	212,237	4	74
Baltimore, Maryland	620,961	5	65.1
Memphis, Tennessee	646,889	6	64.1
New Orleans, Louisiana	343,831	7	61.2
Flint, Michigan	102,434	8	59.5
Montgomery, Alabama	205,764	9	57.4
Savannah, Georgia	136,286	10	56.7

Cities with highest number of Asian-Americans

City	Total population	(Asian-American)	
		Rank	Number
New York, NY	8,175,133	1	1,134,919
Los Angeles, CA	3,792,621	2	483,585
San Jose, CA	945,942	3	326,627
San Francisco, CA	805,235	4	288,529
San Diego, CA	1,307,402	5	241,293
Honolulu, HI	337,256	6	230,071
Chicago, IL	2,695,598	7	166,770

Houston, TX	2,099,451	8	139,960
Fremont, CA	214,089	9	116,755
Philadelphia	1,526,006	10	106,720

Top States with Largest Native American populations:

1. California
2. Oklahoma
3. Arizona
4. New Mexico
5. Texas
6. North Carolina
7. Washington
8. Alaska
9. New York
10. South Dakota

Top Cities with Highest Native American Populations:

- New York, New York
- Los Angeles, California
- Phoenix, Arizona
- Oklahoma City, Oklahoma
- Anchorage, Alaska

US Communities with highest Hispanic-majority populations in 2010 census:

Communities in the United States with a Hispanic-majority population are primarily found in the Southwestern United States and in large metropolitan areas elsewhere in the country.

The community with the highest percentage of Hispanic residents (among communities with over 100,000 people) is the unincorporated community of East Los Angeles, California, whose population was 97.1% Hispanic.

Among incorporated localities of over 100,000 people, the city of Laredo, Texas has the highest percentage of Hispanic residents at 95.6%.

San Antonio, Texas is the largest Hispanic-majority city in the United States, with 807,000 Hispanics making up 61.2% of its population.

New York City has the most Hispanic residents, although it is not Hispanic-majority.

Alaska American Targeted Search – Top 10 Alaska Companies:

1. FORT WAINWRIGHT FEDERAL CREDIT UNION
2. Bristol Bay Native
3. Chugach Alaska
4. Afognak Native
5. Anchorage School District
6. Yukon-Kuskokwim Health
7. Ukpeaġvik Iñupiat
8. Kenai Peninsula Borough School District
9. NANA Dev
10. Lynden

Source: This information was compiled using Wikipedia sources.

Chapter 4: Boolean String Examples:

Talent sourcing involves creating various Boolean strings to find profiles or resumes online. Finding diverse resumes or profiles of candidates can be quite a difficult task. When you think of natural language and the way people introduce themselves online. Gender, Sex, or Race is something that most people do not recognize or mention within their profiles or resumes online.

With that in mind, it is a difficult task when you are trying to source different types of diverse leads.

Including these types of phrases will help direct you to leads.

Examples base on gender:
site:www.linkedin.com/in "machine learning * at" "she|she's|her"

site:facebook.com "minneapolis" "to present" -posts (she or her)

("women who" OR "women in" OR "women for" OR "for women")

"Women Led" (group OR club OR society OR a member OR membership)

(she OR her) (intitle:"resume for" OR intitle:"resume of" OR intitle:"curriculum vitae" OR intitle:"'s resume") -intitle:example -intitle:examples -intitle:sample -intitle:submit

site:meetup.com "member since" women

"is a member of women in technology"

Examples based on race:

(Hispanic OR Latinx OR African American OR Native American)

("africanamerican" OR black OR latino OR latina OR latinx OR hispanic OR "native american" OR "americanindian" OR "alaska native")

How to Search for Attendees at a Conference:
Just include the domain of the conference that you plan to search for and include the string suggestions below:

(intitle:bio OR inurl:bio OR intitle:profile OR inurl:profile OR intitle:homepage OR inurl:homepage OR intitle:"about me" OR inurl:"about me")

(intitle:team OR intitle:staff OR intitle:people OR intitle:employees)

(intitle:attendees OR intitle:members OR intitle:participants OR intitle:registrants OR intitle:roster)

site:nsbe.org intitle:(directory OR list) (attendees OR participants) developer

Here are ways to create Booleans strings to find candidates based on race or gender.

Choose an industry and try and find local communities:

(Latin or Latinx) ("finance" OR CPA" OR "accountant") "sandiego" -samples -jobs

site:about.me "email me" software (developer OR programmer OR engineer OR architect) (Latin OR Latinx) site:www.linkedin.com/in "data scientist" "* * years|experienceof|in|on|with * * * * *"

("africanamerican" OR black OR latino OR latina OR hispanic OR "native american" OR "americanindian" OR "alaska native") (organization OR association OR society)

site:zoominfo.com/p African American site:com

about "minority owned*"

"national society of black engineers"

 site:com "black engineers"

site:diversifytech.co "profiles"

site:twitter.com inurl:with_replies [add keywords] ("Black" OR "Minority" OR "African")

site:meetup.com (java OR python OR ruby OR C# OR C++) "member since" ("Black" OR "African" OR "Latino")

site:reddit.com/r "African" "Engineer*"

site:medium.com/portfolio ("Black" OR "African" OR "African American")

site:medium.com "Also tagged Black Women in Tech"

Search based on Language. Use Google Translate in your search string:

For example:

Email me >envíemeuncorreoelectrónico
My Resume > mi resumen
Seeking opportunities >buscandooportunidades

Or just use the phrase "spanish speaking*"

Alumni Groups
You can search alumni groups and other associations that are connected to diverse groups.

For example:
(NSBE OR "black engineer" OR NSMBA OR "black MBAs" OR AAWIT OR "African American women in technology" OR NAACP OR "black chamber of commerce" OR "African American chamber")

For that search, I was able to quickly put together a list of associations and groups connected this group.
http://nsbc.org/
https://www.blackgirlscode.com/
https://www.blacksintechnology.net/
https://blacktechnation.com/
http://blacktechweek.com/
http://www.code2040.org/
https://www.blackbusiness.com/
http://blacktechwomen.mystrikingly.com/
https://www.colorintech.org/
https://www.devcolor.org/
https://diversityadvocates.com/
https://imblackintech.com/
https://www.thedreamcorps.org/our-programs/tech/
https://www.nacme.org/
https://www.blacktechjobs.com/
https://www.blackwomentalktech.com/
https://blackcodecollective.com/
https://www.aabe.org/
http://www.colorcommnetwork.com/
https://www.elcinfo.com/index.php
https://itsmfonline.org/
https://nbmbaa.org/
https://www.uncf.org/

https://100blackmen.org/

List of Historically Black Universities:
Bowie State University
Clark Atlanta University
Fisk University
Grambling State University
Howard University
Jackson State University
Morehouse College
South Carolina State University
Southern University Baton Rouge
Spelman College
Stillman College
Tuskegee University
Xavier University

I recommended doing an Xray search for career related content and group info.

For example:
site:xavier.edu "alumni"

Meetups Group Example:
Prepare a basic search to find diverse groups and organizations. You can use other tools to scrape and find users within these groups.
https://www.meetup.com/topics/blacks-in-tech/

Locations include: Seattle, New York, Boston, Dallas, Bay Area, Chicago, & LA etc.

Events / Conferences:
("Black" OR "African" OR "African American")
(intitle:attendees OR inurl:attendees OR intitle:participants OR inurl:participants OR intitle:roster OR inurl:roster OR intitle:registrants OR inurl:registrants)

Examples of websites that show up from this search:
https://www.diversifytech.co/events
https://womenofpowertech.blackenterprise.com/
https://afrotech.com/
https://techinclusion.co/
https://www.blacksintechnology.net/
https://www.hireblackmarketers.co/

LinkedIn Groups:
Try searching within LinkedIn Groups. You may be surprised to find a local chapter for a diverse niche that you are trying to recruit for.

Below I've included some examples of Black Technology groups:
https://www.linkedin.com/company/blacks-in-technology/
https://www.linkedin.com/groups/94810/
https://www.linkedin.com/groups/78450/
https://www.linkedin.com/groups/8873861/
https://www.linkedin.com/groups/2238643/
https://www.linkedin.com/groups/8810321/
https://www.linkedin.com/groups/81431/

Facebook Groups:
Try searching directly on Facebook to find groups. Within a quick search, I was able to find this group. You can easily join and network with users within the group. I recommend checking out the Swordfish extension which will give you contact details of individual profiles.

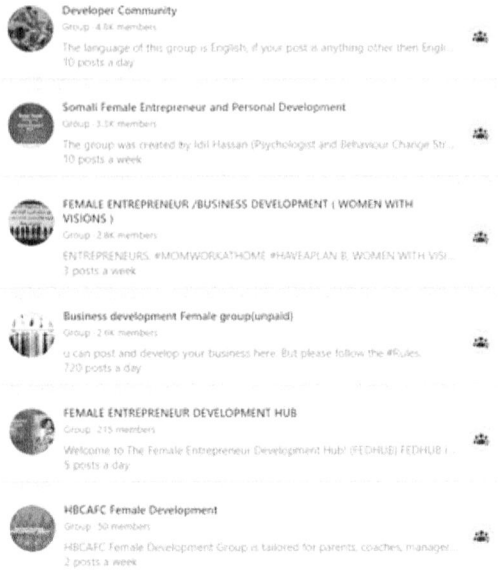

Developer Community
Group · 4.8K members
The language of this group is English, if your post is anything other then Engli...
10 posts a day

Somali Female Entrepreneur and Personal Development
Group · 3.3K members
The group was created by Idil Hassan (Psychologist and Behaviour Change Str...
10 posts a week

FEMALE ENTREPRENEUR /BUSINESS DEVELOPMENT (WOMEN WITH VISIONS)
Group · 2.8K members
ENTREPRENEURS, #MOMWORKATHOME #HAVEAPLAN B, WOMEN WITH VISI...
3 posts a week

Business development Female group(unpaid)
Group · 2.6K members
u can post and develop your business here. But please follow the #Rules.
7/0 posts a day

FEMALE ENTREPRENEUR DEVELOPMENT HUB
Group · 215 members
Welcome to The Female Entrepreneur Development Hub! (FEDHUB) FEDHUB i...
5 posts a day

HBCAFC Female Development
Group · 50 members
HBCAFC Female Development Group is tailored for parents, coaches, manager...
2 posts a week

https://www.facebook.com/blacktechwomen/

Pro tip: You can also scrape Facebook Group data using tools like Phantombuster. Scraping profile data will include a user's name with potential contact information.

Sourcing Tips:
Name generation is a controversial topic within our community. Some have taken offense to this practice of using first names. It does not fully consider all possibilities when searching for a particular race or gender and can be very limiting. I want to be clear that I do not think this is the best tool for finding diverse candidates and do not explicitly endorse it, though it will produce results.

Pro tip: The max searched words within Google is 32 words. However, you can use other websites like LinkedIn and others that do not have a search limit.

The examples below involves using common first names within a race.

Source: https://wizardsourcer.com/top-boolean-strings-to-find-diversity-candidates-online

Top Black Surnames
((williams OR johnson OR smith OR jones OR brown OR jackson OR davis OR thomas OR harris OR robinson OR taylor OR wilson) OR moore OR white OR lewis OR walker OR green OR washington OR thompson OR anderson OR scott OR carter OR wright OR miller OR hill OR allen OR mitchell OR young OR lee OR martin OR clark OR turner OR hall OR king OR edwards OR coleman OR james OR evans OR bell OR richardson OR adams OR brooks OR parker OR jenkins OR stewart OR howard OR campbell OR simmons OR sanders OR henderson OR collins OR cooper OR watson OR butler OR alexander OR bryant OR nelson OR morris OR barnes OR jordan OR reed OR woods OR dixon OR roberts OR gray OR phillips OR griffin OR baker OR powell OR bailey OR ford OR holmes OR banks OR daniels OR ross OR rogers OR perr)

(foster OR patterson OR hunter OR owens OR grant OR marshall OR henry OR morgan OR price OR wallace OR ward OR hayes OR boyd OR freeman OR graham OR hamilton OR franklin OR hawkins OR gordon OR sims OR harrison OR ellis OR kelly OR hicks OR bennett OR joseph OR gibson OR crawford OR jefferson OR watkins OR tucker OR porter OR willis OR mason OR matthews OR fields OR cook OR hughes OR simpson OR hudson OR cole OR warren OR russell OR west OR reid OR murphy OR wells OR mack OR murray OR douglas OR bradley OR frazier OR shaw OR harper OR greene OR robertson OR payne OR perkins OR byrd OR spencer OR webb OR oliver OR cox OR austin OR berry OR lawrence OR mcdonald OR montgomery OR love OR mccoy OR burton OR black OR knight OR harvey OR andrews OR cunningham OR stephens OR armstrong OR peterson OR glover OR long OR haynes OR riley OR hampton OR wade OR miles OR palmer OR neal OR gardner OR ferguson OR garrett)

(tate OR singleton OR hunt OR reynolds OR curry OR charles
OR chambers OR hardy OR hines OR little OR walton OR rice
OR mills OR fisher OR mosley OR caldwell OR booker OR
alston OR carr OR lawson OR roberson OR kennedy OR terry
OR houston OR burns OR mcgee OR ray OR myers OR fuller
OR stevenson OR thornton OR watts OR duncan OR ingram OR
pearson OR gaines OR dorsey OR flowers OR parks OR lane
OR george OR stevens OR stokes OR ware OR dawson OR
reese OR dennis OR francis OR horton OR mckinney OR
holloway OR jennings OR graves OR tyler OR hopkins OR
fleming OR battle OR williamson OR vaughn OR wiggins OR
dunn OR clay OR lucas OR jacobs OR sutton OR floyd OR
pierre OR daniel OR rivers OR malone OR moss OR dean OR
clarke OR chapman OR bush OR logan OR shelton OR bates
OR gibbs OR pierce OR arnold OR holland OR saunders OR
hart OR mccray OR rhodes OR wilkins OR gilbert OR townsend
OR richards OR rodgers OR lowe OR mathis OR morrison OR
nichols OR fletcher OR cannon OR elliott OR rose OR howell
OR anthony OR glenn OR garner OR boone OR pittman OR
dickerson OR norman OR simon OR wheeler OR cobb OR
monroe OR barnett OR branch OR curtis OR lyons OR mcdaniel
OR hubbard OR woodard OR lindsey OR page OR mays OR
bolden OR randolph OR bradford OR copeland OR pitts OR
blake OR sullivan OR chandler OR mcclain OR carroll)

Most Popular African Names
(Imani OR Ebony OR Shanice OR Aaliyah OR Precious OR Nia
OR Deja OR Diamond OR Asia OR Aliyah OR Jada OR Tierra
OR Tiara OR Kiara OR Jazmine OR Jasmin OR Jazmin OR
Jasmine OR Alexus OR Raven)DeShawn OR DeAndre OR
Marquis OR Darnell OR Terrell OR Malik OR Trevon OR
Tyrone OR Willie OR Dominique OR Demetrius OR Reginald
OR Jamal OR Maurice OR Jalen OR Darius OR Xavier OR
Terrance OR Andre OR Darryl)

Top First name with Haitian Origin
("Nanschmide" OR "CATHELINE" OR "ChristelleAnnoa" OR
"Mannuela" OR "Kensia" OR "Myou" OR "wilvarde" OR

"Gaen" OR "hericka" OR "cassanne" OR "ladymia" OR
"ZaÃ¯tuna" OR "Anaica" OR "Nephertarie" OR "johane" OR
"Skay" OR "Ana" OR "lyncees" OR "Dadorie" OR "louis
chritelle" OR "paolita" OR "madelie" OR "rosecarla" OR
"Audrey" OR "Winchell" OR "Skailee" OR "Pharah" OR "aicha"
OR "Eyma" OR "Marlissa" OR Mathilda" OR "sabatina" OR
"nissoue" OR "mc.lane" OR "Daphney" OR "Jalo") OR "keekah"
OR "Louisena" OR "Niquelle" OR "Jennifer" OR "Mitchell-
Sandra" OR "Mina" OR "valencia" OR "Tatiana" OR "Herin"
OR "Aimee" OR "Laetitia" OR "Fredely" OR "Michel" OR
"cristelle" OR "Marylin" OR "Alexa" OR "Chisty" OR "malia"
OR "Gaby" OR "Jasmine" OR "Sandra" OR "michaelle" OR
"Nathaima Lynn-Flaure" OR "lise" OR "TrÃ©cee" OR
"Christelle" OR "Yolanda" OR "Rachelle" OR "Leila" OR
"Betiane" OR "Lourdy" OR "Kerline" OR "louloune" OR
"dedou" OR "LeyssaGaelle" OR "MishaÃ¯na" OR "Shamah"
OR "Emma-Ludmyr" OR "PAÃœLIA" OR "James" OR "Wood"
OR "Emmanuel" OR "stanley" OR "Sidney" OR "Ricardo" OR
"Rims-ky" OR "Davidson colsensky" OR "Kenndhy" OR "richo"
OR "Jhonson" OR "Guelo" OR "Jemmyson" OR "Michel
Olivier" OR "TÃ©maÃ«l" OR "odney" OR "Olgues" OR
"Bernardo" OR "Duckenson" OR "meila" OR "Jules" OR
"Jameson" OR "loovens" OR "Wilkens" OR "Frero" OR "John"
OR "Donald" OR "Begory" OR "Selvandieu" OR "Mti" OR
"jean odly" OR "JEAN ENOCK" OR "Johnny Wolf" OR
"Loubens" OR "Roodney" OR "Carven" OR "stefrey" OR
"Mackendevinci" OR "Jean-Claude" OR "jon" OR "Toussaint"
OR "sylvestre" OR "olson" OR "Ency" OR "CLAJAMES" OR
"JOHN GUYVE" OR "Widmarck" OR "walken" OR "Odelin"
OR "rimpel" OR "young" OR "AKATSUKI" OR "Widnel" OR
"leonaldo" OR "peterlay" OR "Budry" OR "NarumElie" OR
"jean Jackson" OR "Ed Allen" OR "Yves" OR "ANGELO" OR
"Jean wilking" OR "Carl edouard" OR "Makenley" OR "Frandy"
OR "pierre" OR "Dieter Adler" OR "Hercule" OR "Jn Jacques"
OR "Estherson" OR "Lorvensky" OR "Ronaldo" OR "Pierre
stephane" OR "prince-jeyjey" OR "Hans Whalter" OR "Danley"
OR "Zhedd" OR "Burk" OR "Widmy" OR "Arly")

Most Popular African Female Names

(Nia OR Cadence OR Hanna OR Nala OR Zahra OR Zendaya
OR Ayanna OR Ayana OR Nahla OR Ashanti OR Makena OR
Dalia OR Za'Niyah OR Ayah OR Nyah OR Candice OR Niyah
OR Ny'asia OR Kaliah OR Iyana OR Niah OR Ka'Mya OR Nya
OR Jahzara OR Laiken OR Nalah OR Tahiry OR Kiya OR
Tanisha OR Keisha OR Zaniya OR Adanna OR Ka'Liyah OR
Lakeisha OR Nisha OR Zehra OR Kamile OR Eshal OR Shade
OR Nokutenda OR Evte OR Amrit OR Tinaye)

105 HCBU's:
("Alabama A&M University" OR "Alabama State University"
OR "Albany State University" OR "Alcorn State University" OR
"Allen University" OR "University of Arkansas at Pine Bluff"
OR "Arkansas Baptist College" OR "Barber-Scotia College" OR
"Benedict College" OR "Bennett College" OR "Bethune-
Cookman University" OR "Bishop State Community College"
OR "Bluefield State College" OR "Bowie State University" OR
"Central State University" OR "Cheyney University of
Pennsylvania" OR "Claflin University" OR "Clark Atlanta
University" OR "Clinton Junior College" OR "Coahoma
Community College" OR "Concordia College, Selma" OR
"Coppin State University" OR "Delaware State University" OR
"Denmark Technical College" OR "Dillard University" OR
"University of the District of Columbia" OR "Edward Waters
College" OR "Elizabeth City State University" OR "Fayetteville
State University" OR "Fisk University" OR "Florida A&M
University" OR "Florida Memorial University" OR "Fort Valley
State University" OR "Gadsden State Community College" OR
"Grambling State University" OR "Hampton University" OR
"Harris-Stowe State University" OR "Hinds Community College
at Utica" OR "Howard University" OR "Huston-Tillotson
University" OR "Interdenominational Theological Center" OR
"J. F. Drake State Technical College" OR "Jackson State
University" OR "Jarvis Christian College" OR "Johnson C.
Smith University" OR "Kentucky State University" OR
"Knoxville College" OR "Lane College" OR "Langston
University" OR "Lawson State Community College" OR
"LeMoyne-Owen College" OR "Lewis College of Business" OR
"Lincoln University" OR "Lincoln University of Missouri" OR

"Livingstone College" OR "University of Maryland Eastern Shore" OR "Meharry Medical College" OR "Miles College" OR "Mississippi Valley State University" OR "Morehouse College" OR "Morehouse School of Medicine" OR "Morgan State University" OR "Morris Brown College" OR "Morris College" OR "Norfolk State University" OR "North Carolina A&T State University" OR "North Carolina Central University" OR "Oakwood University" OR "Paine College" OR "Paul Quinn College" OR "Philander Smith College" OR "Prairie View A&M University" OR "Rust College" OR "Saint Paul's College" OR "Savannah State University" OR "Selma University" OR "Shaw University" OR "Shorter College" OR "Shelton State Community College" OR "South Carolina State University" OR "Southern University at New Orleans" OR "Southern University at Shreveport" OR "Southern University and A&M College" OR "Southwestern Christian College" OR "Spelman College" OR "St. Augustine's College" OR "St. Philip's College" OR "Stillman College" OR "Talladega College" OR "Tennessee State University" OR "Texas College" OR "Texas Southern University" OR "Tougaloo College" OR "Trenholm State Technical College" OR "Tuskegee University" OR "University of the Virgin Islands" OR "Virginia State University" OR "Virginia Union University" OR "Virginia University of Lynchburg" OR "Voorhees College" OR "West Virginia State University" OR "Wilberforce University" OR "Wiley College" OR "Winston-Salem State University" OR "Xavier University of Louisiana")

African American Fraternities & Sororities.
"Sigma Pi Phi" OR "Alpha Phi Alpha" OR "Kappa Alpha Psi" OR "Omega Psi Phi" OR "Phi Beta Sigma" OR "Sigma Rhomeo" OR "Wine Psi Phi" OR "Iota Phi Theta" OR "Phi Delta Psi" OR "Delta Psi Chi" OR "Beta Phi Pi" OR "MALIK Fraternity" OR "Sigma Phi Rho" OR "Phi Rho Eta" OR "Gamma Psi Beta" OR "Alpha Kappa Alpha" OR "Delta Sigma Theta" OR "Zeta Phi Beta" OR "Sigma Gamma Rho" OR "Phi Delta Kappa" OR "Iota Phi Lambda" OR "Eta Phi Beta" OR "Gamma Phi Delta")

More African Baby Names in 2020
(Abioye OR Adebowale OR Adisa OR Afia OR Afolabi OR
Afua OR Akachi OR Akinyi OR Akua OR Amaka OR Amara
OR Amare OR Anaya OR Arusi OR Ashanti OR Ayana OR Ayo
OR Ayodele OR Ayotunde OR Baako OR Babajide OR
Babatunde OR Berko OR Boipelo OR Bongani OR Bosede OR
Cayman OR Chibuzo OR Chidike OR Chidubem OR Chike OR
Chikelu OR Chikere OR Chipo OR Chuks OR Chukwuemeka
OR Dakarai OR Dayo OR Deka OR Delu OR Desta OR
Dikeledi OR Dubaku OR Ebele OR Efua OR Ekua OR Emeka
OR Emem OR Faraji OR Femi OR Folami OR Fumnaya OR
Furaha OR Ife OR Imani OR Imari OR Jabari OR Jaheem OR
Jaz OR Jelani OR Jojo OR Kanye OR Katlego OR Keyon OR
Khari OR Kofi OR Kojo OR Kunto OR Kwame OR Kwanza OR
Lekan OR Lerato)

Keywords
"Africa Business Club" OR "Kappa Alpha Psi" OR "Men of God
Christian Fraternity" OR "National Association of Black
Telecom Professionals" OR "National Association of Colored
People" OR "National Multicultural Greek Council" OR
"National Pan-Hellenic Council" OR "National Pan-Hellenic
Council" OR "Omega Psi Phi" OR "Phi Beta Sigma" OR "Phi
Delta Psi" OR "Sigma Gamma Rho" OR "The Black Patriots
Foundation" OR "The HBCU Network" OR "The National Black
Graduate Student Association" OR "Zeta Phi Beta" OR
"National Society of Black Engineers (NSBE)" OR "National
Society of Black Engineers" OR "National Society of Black
Engineers (NSBE)" OR "National Society of Black Engineers"
OR "Society of Black Scientists and Engineers (HSBSE)" OR
"National Society of Black Engineers (NSBE)" OR "National
Society of Black Engineers" OR "Society of Black Scientists and
Engineers (SBSE)" OR "National Society of Black Engineers
(NSBE) " OR "Black Engineering and Science Student
Association (BESSA)" OR "Organization of African-American
Students Excelling in STEM (OASES)" OR "Black Graduate
Student Association" OR "National Society of Black Engineers
(NSBE)" OR "Black Engineers Society" OR "National Society

of Black Engineers" OR "National Society of Black Engineers - NSBE" OR "National Society of Black Engineers"

Orgs:
"Africa Business Club" OR "Kappa Alpha Psi" OR "Men of God Christian Fraternity" OR "National Association of Black Telecom Professionals" OR "National Association of Colored People" OR "National Multicultural Greek Council" OR "National Pan-Hellenic Council" OR "National Pan-Hellenic Council" OR "Omega Psi Phi" OR "Phi Beta Sigma" OR "Phi Delta Psi" OR "Sigma Gamma Rho" OR "The Black Patriots Foundation" OR "The HBCU Network" OR "The National Black Graduate Student Association" OR "Zeta Phi Beta"

Top Black Professional Organization from Wikipedia
("100 Blacks in Law Enforcement Who Care" OR "Afro-American Patrolmen's League" OR "Association of Black Psychologists" OR "Association of Black Sociologists" OR "Association of Black Women Historians" OR "The Barristers' Association of Philadelphia" OR "Black Data Processing Associates" OR "Cook County Bar Association" OR "Georgia Alliance of African American Attorneys" OR "International Association of Black Actuaries" OR "Metropolitan Black Bar Association" OR "National Association for Black Veterans" OR "National Association of Black Accountants" OR "National Association of Black Geologists and Geophysicists" OR "National Association of Black Journalists" OR "The National Association of Blacks in Criminal Justice" OR "National Association of Colored Graduate Nurses" OR "National Bar Association" OR "National Black Chamber of Commerce" OR "National Black Farmers Association" OR "National Black Law Students Association" OR "National Black MBA Association" OR "National Black Nurses Association" OR "National Black Police Association (United States)" OR "National Conference of Black Lawyers" OR "National Dental Association" OR "National Insurance Association" OR "National Medical Association" OR "National Negro Bar Association" OR "National Negro Business League" OR "National Organization for the Professional Advancement of Black Chemists and

Chemical Engineers" OR "National Organization of Black Women in Law Enforcement" OR "National Society of Black Engineers" OR "National Society of Black Physicists" OR "The Organization of Black Designers" OR "Philadelphia Association of Black Journalists" OR "Progressive Black & Journalists" OR "Student National Medical Association" OR "Washington Bar Association")

Pro tip: Wikipedia and Acronymfinder.com use these two search engines to find different terms, associations, colleges, or associations.

University and College
("africanamerican" OR black OR "latino" OR "Latina" OR hispanic OR "latinx" OR "native american" OR "americanindian" OR "alaska native") engineer (colleges OR schools OR universities)

Non-Profits
Many nonprofits focus on diverse groups. You can find groups within different industries like Finance, HR, Marketing, and Technology.

/dev/color
National Black Engineers
ColorStack
Techqueria
Latinas in Tech
Latina Professionals™
Underrepresented Minorities in Computing
Diversifytech.co
Womenwho.design
Blackswho.design
Latinxswhodesign.com
Blackswho.engineer
Talent.nativesintech.org

Affinity Groups

Larger companies have internal diverse groups that you can search for.
(IBM OR Microsoft OR Google OR Facebook) employee (affinity OR "resource group")

1. Google

Women@Google, Hispanic Googlers Network (HOLA), Black Googlers Network, Trans at Google, Gayglers, & Google American Indian Network.

2. Microsoft

Women@Microsoft, Blacks@Microsoft (BAM), GLEAM (Global LGBTQIA+ Employees and Allies at Microsoft), &Hispanic/Latinx Organization of Leaders in Action (HOLA)

3. Facebook

Women@, Black@, Latin@, Pride@, &Native@.

4. Uber

LadyEng, UberMosaic, Los Ubers, UberHue, Women of Uber, &UberPride.

5. Lyft

UpLyft Women, UpLyft Forward, LyftOut, &UpLyftUnidos.

6. Amazon

Glam, Asians@Amazon, Black Employee Network, Indigenous@Amazon, Latinos@Amazon, Warriors@Amazon, Women@Amazon, &Women in Finance Initiative

Searching for Layoff Lists

Many candidates have been impacted by layoffs in recent months. Here's a guide on how to find layoff lists online using Boolean strings.

With so many companies furloughing and laying off employees, it's a good time to search and find active talent open for their next opportunity. As Recruiters, we are researchers, so I wanted to give some tips and tricks for finding layoff lists or announcements online. Let's use our super powers to find some great talent online! Here's some advice for finding layoff lists.

1. Search Hashtags on Social Media sites

Many leads are turning to social media during these tough times to both vent about their tough situations and even actively seek out new job opportunities. You can find these leads by using the right hashtags on platforms like Twitter, Facebook, and even Instagram. LinkedIn also supports the use of hashtags, and that's a great place to start.

When searching for hashtags, consider tags like #jobsearching, #jobseeking, #furlough, #layoffs, and so on. You can also add a location to your search and this will help you narrow down results to your specific location so that you can find leads more easily.

Here's an example that I found doing a hashtag search on Twitter:

The Uber and Airbnb Alumni lists published to help them find new jobs might become the new standard for mass layoffs:

Uber: https://coda.io/@kenny/uber-layoff-list

Airbnb: https://airbnb.com/d/talent

2. Set Google Alerts

There is all sorts of news coming out regarding layoffs and major changes at some of the world's biggest companies. As a recruiter, you should stay on top of these things. So, set Google Alerts so that you get notified whenever a new article is posted regarding job layoffs.

When you set a Google Alert, you can create it for any number of search terms. For these purposes, it's a good idea to setup Google Alerts for terms like "layoff list" and so on. Google will then notify you via email as often as you desire (a daily summary will likely be best) and you can skim the new results regularly.

3. Layoff Boolean String Examples

A Google search can reveal all sorts of helpful information, but you have to be using the right search terms just like you have to be using the right hashtags on social media. Boolean search strings on Google docs, for instance, will help you find excel lists and more that consider specific wording.

site:docs.google.com/ "layoff list*"

Doing a quick search with this string the first doc that comes up is a Crypto Layoff list with 30+ names listed.

Another example is looking for layoff news; you can search Google news with this string: ("Laid off" OR "Layoff*" OR "Laying off"). If you're not already familiar with using Boolean search strings, it's worth looking into because they are major time savers. Not only can you get very specific about what results you want to see, but you can also get results for multiple search terms at once.

4. Make Use of Tracking Tools

Keeping on top of how your company is being talked about can help you find potential leads, too. Anyone who mentions your company may be interested in an opportunity, so tracking your company's mentions is worthwhile. I've included a full list of monitoring tools (here).

You can use variety to tools to do this while also tracking social media mentions and hashtags, monitoring inbound and outbound mentions, and using tools like Open Site Explorer to analyze inbound links to your company's website etc.

5. Researching News

Use these websites to monitor and track related news and press release updates.

Owler: It crowd-sources competitive insights by providing news alerts, company profiles, and polls and allows members to follow, track, and research companies in real-time.

Crunchbase: Is a platform for finding business information about private and public companies. The site includes investments and funding information, founding members and individuals in leadership positions, mergers and acquisitions, news, and industry trends

HackerNews: Is a social news website focusing on computer science and entrepreneurship.

It's a news aggregator forum site similar to Reddit, but it primarily focuses on start-ups, developers, and hacker related news. Topics include anything that "good hackers" would find interesting. Founded by Paul Graham, he wanted to create a community that would recreate the way Reddit felt in the good old days when developers were the main focus.

While reviewing the site, I found out that Hacker News created a sub specifically for developers actively looking for new opportunities. This sub is a month by month page called: Ask HN: Who wants to be hired?

The information included in this sub:

- Name:
- Location:
- Remote:
- Willing to relocate:
- Technologies:
- Résumé/CV:
- Email:

You can create a Boolean string to find talent:

Ask HN: Who wants to be hired? ("October" OR "September" OR "November" OR "December" OR "January") AND "2019"

Layoff News Tech Communities:

Roof Top Slushie: Helps you connect with employees at top tech companies like Google and Facebook. Get job interview tips, career advice, insights, and more

Team Blind: Is an anonymous community app for the workplace. Our vision in creating this space was to break down professional barriers and hierarchy.

Google News: Is a news aggregator app developed by Google. It presents a continuous, customizable flow of articles organized from thousands of publishers and magazines.

TheLayoff: Is a site where users can list layoff updates anonymously.

This section will cover how to search and Xray individual Social media sites and other websites online:

LinkedIn Search

LinkedIn is the top places to find a diverse group of talent online.

Diversity Sourcing takes practice and patience as a Recruiter. LinkedIn is a great place to find available diverse (BLNA) profiles. In this post, I will highlight the main features within LinkedIn Recruiter and give Boolean String examples to find diverse profiles.

First, I wanted to cover some basics and tips and tricks on how to perform searches within LinkedIn Recruiter. LinkedIn itself has a great deal of learning videos and content for you to get familiarized on the platform. The following discussion assumes familiarity with the platform, and it is best to have LinkedIn Recruiter search page open side by side along with this guide.

How to run a search in LinkedIn Recruiter:

Use Job Titles filter for functional and analytical roles as opposed to developer or heavily technical roles. Titles that are the most effective are, for example: Project or Program Managers, Technical Program Managers, Software Development Managers, Business Systems Analyst, Data Analyst, Data Engineers, or Quality Assurance Analyst titles.

Titles that least effective are: Any developer related or Software Engineering types of roles since they are more keywords and hard skills driven.

Job titles

enter a job title or boolean...

Include:

- ● Current or Past
- ○ Current
- ○ Past not Current
- ○ Past

The Locations filter is straight forward. It is a good idea to always start a local search before expanding into a national search.

Locations

enter a location...

Include:

- ● Current
- ○ Current or open to relocate
- ○ Open to relocate only

Skills filter is an important one since this is where you input your required skills from the requirement. LinkedIn auto-populates commonly used or related skills, but you can always enter the skills manually. The Skills section also supports Boolean Strings and treats multiple inputs as OR statements by default.

Note: Skills filter ONLY searches for the skills section of someone's LinkedIn profile (see example below) rather than the entirety of the profile. If a candidate didn't list a specific skill in the Skills section but rather in other parts of the profile, you will not likely find that candidate based on Skills search alone.

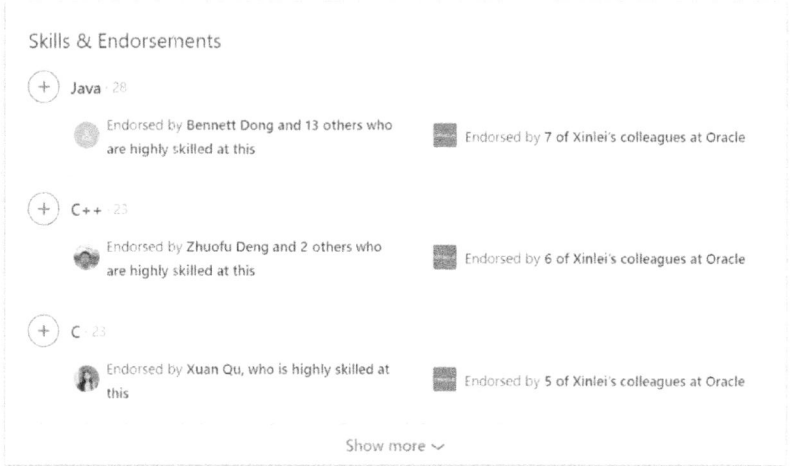

Companies filter produces the most value if you are targeting talent coming from a specific company. This filter is also useful in EXCLUDING candidates from other companies.

Keywords filter is the MOST IMPORTANT filter and the most powerful one. This is where you can input your own Boolean strings with relevant terms and LinkedIn will scan a candidate's entire profile to look for keyword matches and pull up the results accordingly.

This is the place that gives you the most amount of control on how you want the searches to be done outside of Job Title and Skills filters. You can input literally anything in this section from skills, to schools, to associations, and to responsibilities. Think outside the box when searching for diverse leads.

Pro tip: You can have LinkedIn search based on individual user's profiles. Just include the users name within the search bar and it will pull all the keywords. This helps when you are looking for more diverse leads – will help suggest similar profiles in a search.

You cannot search for "race" or "gender" within LinkedIn Recruiter, but you can look for groups, associations, nonprofits, locations, universities where these candidates might attend for example:

(NSBE OR "black engineer" OR NSMBA OR "black MBAs" OR AAWIT OR "African American women in technology" OR NAACP OR "black chamber of commerce" OR "African American chamber")

Add Colleges and Universities that are known for having diverse students:

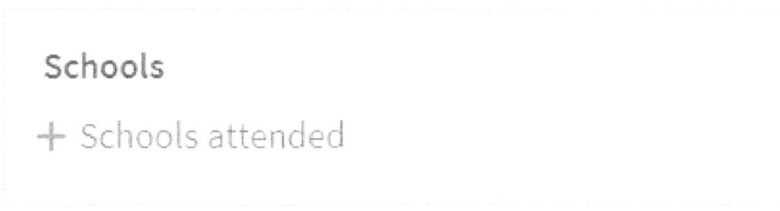

Creating LinkedIn Projects

If you are happy or satisfied with a search, create a project on LinkedIn and name it. Once you have a project created, you can save your search by clicking on the Ribbon next to the trash can icon. Enter a search name and select the Project name you have created for this search and hit save.

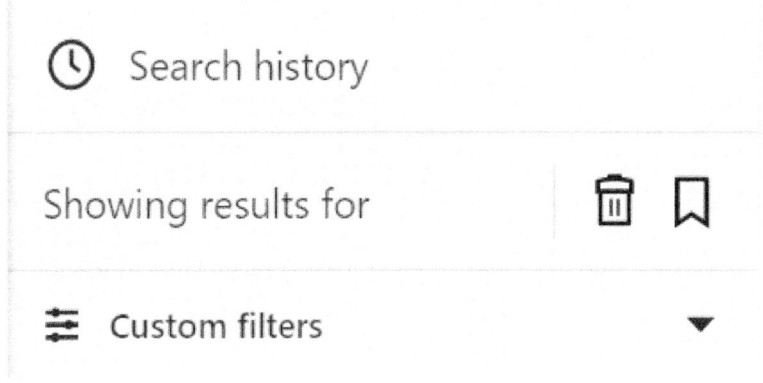

Pro tip from Guillaume Alexandre: The one technique I developed that works well though, is to make a generic search for your skills keywords and add all people who seem to fit your diversity target into a project. Recreate your search, excluding your project over and over again until your project is full of only diverse candidates.

This is a great little feature when you have been running the same search multiple times and want to look at fresh candidates. Check the Hide previous viewed box and set a timeframe between 3 or 6 months to pull up results that you have NOT viewed before.

Hide previously viewed   Past 3 months   ▼

Not viewed

Setting up automatic LinkedIn alerts to let LinkedIn source for you AUTOMATICALLY and push new candidates directly to you via email alerts for any saved searches that you do consistently.

Network Relationships filter allows you to search people based on the search criteria. 1st relationships are someone you have connected with and 2nd relationships are you have a common connection and 3rd relationships are everyone else. It is recommended to do searches within 1st connections first because you can directly message these people and get a better response rate and then search 2nd connections using your common connection as a warmer intro. InMail feature provides the most value with a Recruiter License on 3rd connections, but this is where response rates can suffer as anyone with a LinkedIn Recruiter License can InMail any 1st, 2nd, OR 3rd connections.

Network relationships

1st Connections (2K+)

2nd Connections (1.3M+)

Group Members (1M+)

3rd + Everyone Else (640M+)

Search Similar Profiles

LinkedIn's matching algorithm will suggest similar profiles based on connections and keyword terms. When you do find a diverse profile, use this feature to find additional connections.

Google Doc Search

Google Docs is a free resource created by Google to help asset users in so many different ways. For example, it can help with content, to creating presentations, to working in (excel) sheets. It something that I use on a weekly basis to work on many different types of projects. Google Docs is a great way to auto-save and maybe it's the one thing you didn't notice. Documents or projects can be saved and viewed publicly online. With the help of Boolean and x-raying Recruiters and search across a ton of public content. You can virtually search endless amounts of content. But, for Recruiters searching for resumes, books, patents, or presentations can help discover more candidates online.

Below are creative ways to source within Google Docs:

Source: https://wizardsourcer.com/creative-ways-to-source-in-google-docs

1. Basic Boolean String to Find Resumes:

I recommend creating a basic string to find resumes. I would start my searching for a particular job title and then expand on require skills and preferred locations. Below is an example for searching Google Docs for resume titles.

---

site:docs.google.com developer "San Francisco" resume -example -sam 🎤 🔍

All   News   Images   Videos   Maps   More   Settings   Tools

About 619 results (0.72 seconds)

rplevy-resume - Google Docs
https://docs.google.com/document/d/12Ip4gT_Vfi0Gd2k7ifXFlpJWZLoqr-8Uh.../edit
r.p.levy@gmail.com | 632 Hyde St. #3, San Francisco, CA, 94109 | 415-800-2951 ... CLOJURE
DEVELOPER, Sonian, Dedham, MA / San Francisco, CA.

Resume: Kristin Erickson - Google Docs
https://docs.google.com/a/ucsc.edu/document/d/.../edit?usp=sharing
Programmer - Artist - Technician - Performer. Address: ... 2015 Lead iOS Developer Wribbn ... HTML,
JSP, Java, JavaScript, CSS, MySQL, San Francisco, CA.

CV - Google Docs
https://docs.google.com/document/d/1Z1jYvQ-U-2M_zERzAn4YRXjkCT3CrjD.../edit
Senior software **developer** based in London with over 10 years commercial ... a number of conferences,
including the Paho/MQTT interop day in San Francisco ...

Sujee Maniyam ES - Resume - Google Docs
https://docs.google.com/document/d/1PBnQY.../edit
San Francisco Bay Area, USA | LinkedIn | GitHub | portfolio | online **resume** | ... Cloudera Certified
Hadoop **Developer**; Hortonworks Certified Hadoop **Developer** ...

Resume software engineer summary - Google Docs
https://docs.google.com/.../d/1tLbJl_yDSbhBlVtrcUyV5aotKnjEiakTE1euigETZ_o/

(Advanced) Resume Boolean String Examples:

I've included more advanced searches that expand on resume keywords. I've also included a string that strictly focused on finding accounts that include Gmail address info.

site:docs.google.com developer "San Francisco" intitle:resume -example -sample -samples –jobs

site:docs.google.com developer Atlanta (intitle:resume OR intitle:cv) -example -sample -samples -jobs

site:docs.google.com developer "San Francisco" (resume OR CV OR "curriculum vitae") -example –

sample -samples -jobs

site:docs.google.com developer "* * @gmail.com" -example -sample -samples –jobs

2. Searching in Documents

This example will help search with the document folders within Google Docs. Users can save documents within these folders.

site:docs.google.com/document/ developer "San Francisco" intitle:resume -example -sample -samples -jobs

3. Searching in Spreadsheets

Spreadsheets are similar to an Excel document. You can search for directories, participants, to conference attendees list. Just consider what someone might create within a spreadsheet and create a string.

site:docs.google/com/spreadsheets/ developer (contacts OR participants OR directory OR registrants OR attendees) – example

site:docs.google.com/spreadsheets / "staff directory" -example

4. Searching in Forms

Forms are documents that showcase survey information. You can search for names and other info that someone might ask within a survey. You can search for participant names, list directories, and other company data Intel.

site:docs.google.com/spreadsheets/ Responses (contacts OR participants OR directory OR

registrants OR attendees) -example

site:docs.google.com/spreadsheets/ Responses "email * * com|net|org" -example

site:docs.google.com/spreadsheets/ "List of *" (contacts OR participants OR directory OR

registrants OR attendees) -example

5. Searching in Presentations

You can search for topics and find individuals who have presented within the space. It's virtually endless for what you could search for within Presentations.

site:docs.google.com/presentation/ docker -example

site:docs.google.com/presentation/ docker "email * *" -example

site:docs.google.com/presentation/ "organizational chart" - example

Pinterest Search

Do you need a creative outlet to find diverse candidates online? Pinterest is a community of creative individuals, many of whom happen to be female and diverse. Below I will show you how to recruit and source them on Pinterest.

There is no doubt that social media is filled with talented people roaming around and Pinterest is no exception. It is a great platform to reach the best talent out there. It is currently the third most popular social network. If you want to show off your company to a diverse pool of potential candidates and advertise your job openings, then Pinterest is a great place use in your recruiting strategy.

Here's the some Statistics on Pinterest's Users:

1. Pinterest has over 320 million active users in 2019 (via sprout social).

2. 71% of active users are female (via Statista).

3. Pinterest users actively research purchases. This also includes potential applicants researching company brands online.

4. The average time spent on Pinterest is 14.2 minutes (via Pinterest).

Here are several ways to use Pinterest in recruiting talent:

1. Sourcing within Pinterest

Unfortunately, search modifiers, operators, Xray strings do not work on Pinterest. They removed the ability to search for profile usernames awhile back. Instead, I would recommend using Pinterest's internal search bar to find users, pins, and pin board suggestions.

2. Building a Pinboard for your Company

If you have job openings in different departments, create a different board for each. Mention the specifics and requirements for the candidate on each board. It will make it easier for the candidates to find the content related to the areas they are interested in. You can use images, hashtags, and keywords to make it prominent. You should redirect the candidates to the website where the job description is posted.

3. Pin Multimedia Content

Pinterest is a lot more than just posting images and waiting for the candidates to apply. You can also pin multimedia there such as your YouTube channel where you can pin videos of the environment at the workplace and more. You can also pin QR codes that help the candidate to get access to the job application easily and quickly.

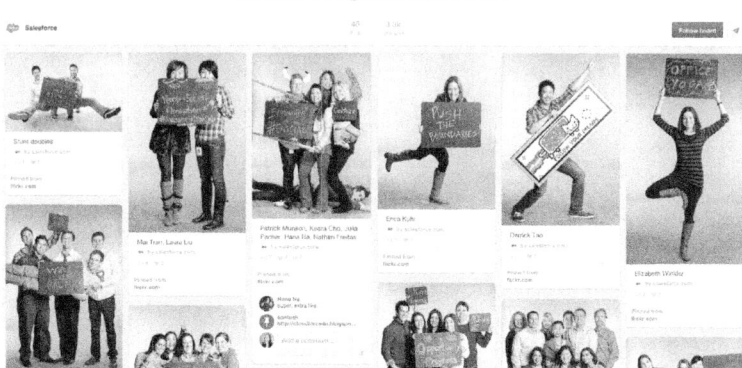

4. Boost your Employment Branding Efforts

Pinterest is a great platform where you can show what working with you is like rather than explain in words. You can share pictures of your workplace and show how people work there. There might be some images of the events you organized or some normal routine daily photos that show you relaxing and entertaining your work environment is. Also, you can add employee testimonials to give a promising image of your company.

5. Connect with your Niche Audience

Though Pinterest doesn't allow you to directly connect with other people it does let you invite people to other places where they can talk and connect. You can redirect the conversation to LinkedIn, where you can have a conversation with them. You ought to give at least one source of communication.

I recommend advertising your employment brand or job posts using Pinterest's advertisement platform. Pinterest has a great community of diverse leads – why not advertise directly to them?

We know what people look for when they open Pinterest. They want to see what is new in fashion, attractive traveling spots or find latest trends, etc. You can relate these trends with your company in several ways such as you can share several outfits best for office wear, or you can share the traveling spots where you took your team for a trip. It is all about being creative with the information that you have.

Instagram Search

Instagram has a Billion monthly users and roughly 52% of those are female. When competition is tough, you need to go where the talent goes. Instagram is a great resource to find and recruit tech-savvy users within major cities across the globe.

The way Instagram is structured is by users, followers, posts, following within the URLs. So, when creating different Boolean strings, it will be to use these terms when manipulating a search string. You can choose internally on Instagram for People, Tags, or Places as well.

Most public profiles include some info:

- Job titles or company info.
- Where they work.
- Where they live.
- Which companies they follow.
- Events and conferences they follow.
- Other interests within the field.

Here's some Boolean String examples:

site:instagram.com "computer science" post followers following

site:instagram.com "software developer" (saint paul or minneapolis) -jobs -inurl:company

site:instagram.com "UX designer" (minneapolis or mn) -jobs -inurl:company site:instagram.com ("content marketing" OR "inbound marketing" OR "content writer" OR "Demand Generation" OR "Content Marketer") ("new york" OR nyc)

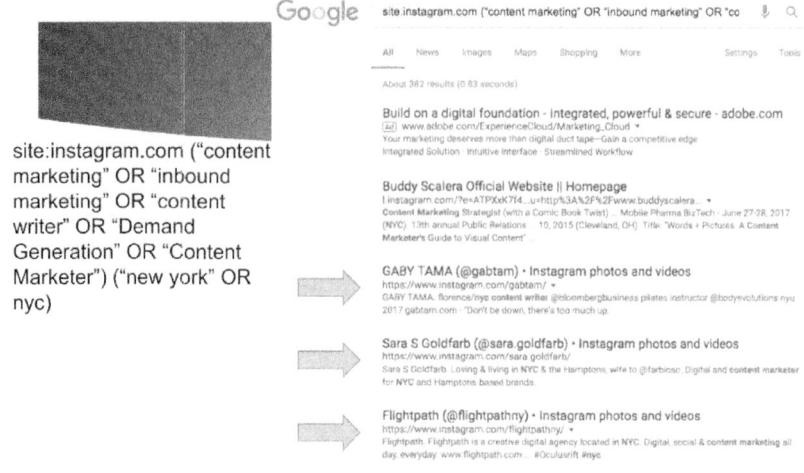

More Creative Ideas:

- You can follow trending hashtags and discover the most active users within a city. (See below)
- If users are using a hashtag for a conference or event, try and connect with them.
- Spy on your competition. If there's a recruiter local to your niche odds are they are connecting and following professionals within that niche.
- Try using Facebook and Instagram ads to different likes or applications to your roles.

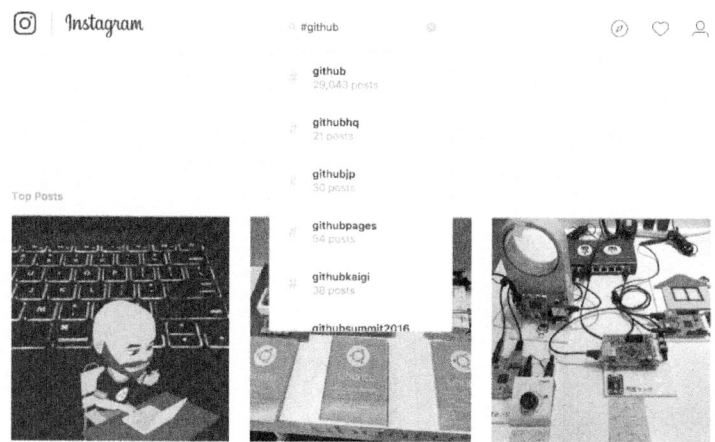

Direct Messaging Profiles:

There are many ways to find a user's email address and I've written about that in other posts. When it comes to DMing profiles I've included some ideas below:

- Being clear and direct with your message.
- Don't jump right into talking about a job.
- Connect on different interests or topics in common.
- Highlight industry and projects connected to them.
- Direct the conversation off the platform and into an email.

SearchMyBio(Tool)

This site is another great option for searching for public profiles. You can search for profile bio information, filter by followers, and connect with the most active users on Instagram. This tool has many other advanced features worth reviewing further.

Employer Branding Ideas:

Outside of directly sourcing you can also use Instagram as a way to promote your company's brand. Here are some creative and unique ways to engage with users:

- Sharing your company's culture and environment.
- Sharing conferences and job fair event news.
- Sharing openings and recent recruiting news.
- Share a project that you are working on! (See Below)

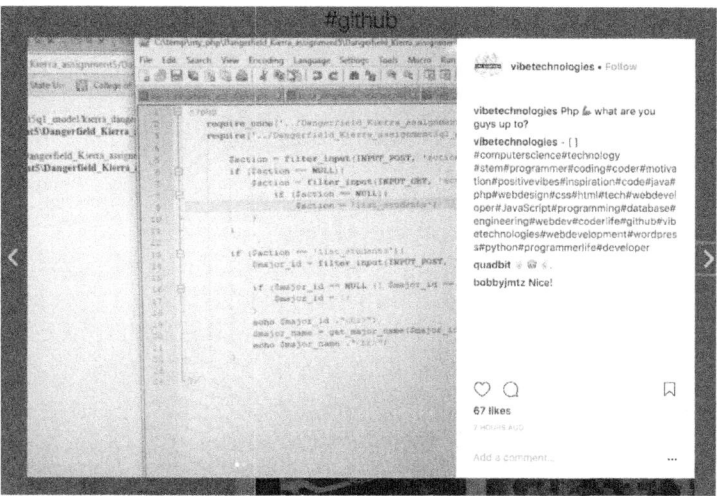

Facebook Search

Facebook is an untapped gold mine when it comes to recruiting and sourcing talent across the web. Basically, it's a massive database of millions of people. The trouble is, many recruiters don't know how to approach using it for such. I wanted to create a basic guide into the world of sourcing Facebook.

Facebook Recruiting Stats from Mashable:

- 85% of internet users have Facebook accounts
- 84% of job seekers have a Facebook profile
- 74% of internet users use Facebook daily
- 57% of Facebook users have 100+ friends
- 58% of Facebook users have liked a brand

Below is a step-by-step guide that will help empower you to source on Facebook.

1. Sourcing Public Profiles

Use the Facebook search option to find users (and company pages) that may represent potential candidates. With powerful search functions, you can find people based on location, work experience, education, employers, and even languages.

Unfortunately, Facebook Graph Search was shut down in August 2019. You can still search for basic things on Facebook. Once you find someone, reach out to them via Facebook or cross-reference their information to find them on LinkedIn or another platform. Don't panic – there's a tool to do graph searches here >https://graph.tips/beta

Boolean Strings:
site:facebook.com "teacher" OR "minneapolis" "to present" - posts

site:facebook.com "software engineer" "to present" -posts "Pittsburgh" ("her" OR "she")

To narrow the search you can include other terms: Latinx, African, Native, Alaskan, Mexican, or Somali.

How to DM someone:

Keep it short and sweet. Don't go into too much detail on the exact openings. Rather, treat Facebook like a relationship-building tool. Try and connect with them on various topics and try and build a connection through similar interests. Don't treat the platform like LinkedIn.

Maybe you didn't realize this by this platform has a desktop version called: Messenger.com. Once you log into this, you will see a large dashboard of all your recent Facebook messages. You search and directly connect with public users on Facebook.

Hang out anytime, anywhere

Messenger makes it easy and fun to stay close to your favorite people.

Continue as Jonathan Kidder

Here's the unique part of this Platform:

1. You can directly search within the search bar and contact users directly.

2. You can search not only user names but cell phone numbers to find active accounts.

3. Messages get directly sent to users and not to the other inbox.

4. Notifications get sent as a text message or pop-up notifications on user's phones.

How can you use Facebook Messenger:

1. Reach out directly to leads that have a public Facebook profile.

2. Be direct and honest with your message right away.

3. Make sure you state the reason for the message.

4. I recommend reaching out to leads AFTER normal business hours.

Shannon Pritchett advises that you use your first message to come clean and confess that Facebook isn't the most appropriate platform for a professional, work-related conversation, admit to stalking them on LinkedIn and suggest carrying the conversation on via email.

Recruiter Facebook Template example:

Hey (Name), I wanted to take a chance and send you a message. I was reviewing your rep scores within github and I was really impressed by your project at Code42. I'm a local Recruiter in the Minneapolis and wanted to introduce myself. What's a good way to connect with your further? Email?

Thanks, Jonathan

2. Create a Facebook Page

Likely, you already have a corporate page with your company that you can use to recruit on Facebook, but you can also open a new profile and start a brand new page, known as your company's "Career" page. The Career page will host content targeted entirely towards people potentially interested in a job, separating the recruiting side from the corporate side, which is targeted at your company's clients.

3. Establish a Company Culture (Employer Brand)

Your company's work culture will do major things for your employer brand. Use your Career page to showcase your company's wonderful work culture and have your employees share their own experiences. This will turn into a form of social recruitment where people will reach out to you wanting to interact with your company solely because of how your photos, videos, and stories portray the culture there. I recommend connecting with Work4labs. They have many Facebook career page tools and products.

4. Launch a Recruiting Ad

While writing a great Facebook ad deserves a guide within itself, this concept is definitely one you should look into. Launching a Facebook recruiting campaign will allow you to quickly and effectively reach targeted groups of people, enabling you to reach as many potential candidates as possible. Some of the best advice you can take when using this method is injecting all the personality you can into your campaign. Remember the importance of employer branding.

5. Promote Your Job Ad

Many people don't realize that they can promote their Facebook job ad for free. Aside from sharing it on your Facebook page, you can also share it with relevant Facebook groups where you should frequently talk about your employer brand and recruitment opportunities. Additionally, you can have your partners and colleagues share the ad themselves, helping it reach even more people.

Another free way to promote a recruitment opportunity is with Facebook Marketplace. The Marketplace is where people go to buy and sell items within their community, and while there is no dedicated category for job listings, many savvy recruiters are already using it to find candidates.

6. Use Facebook Live

Finally, another under-utilized tactic when reporting on Facebook is the Facebook Live feature. With this feature, you can use live chats on your Career page along with a live video to introduce your team, explain various recruitment opportunities, and answer candidates' questions, all while engaging them in a very lively way. Best of all, this tactic is completely free as well!

Reddit Search

You may have heard of the popular online forum Reddit.com as a go to place to get answers to your questions or find the latest news stories. One area you may not have associated with the fourth largest website online today is its potential for recruiting. Yes, you can use Reddit to source and recruit potential candidates online.

Millennials and technology gurus use this site daily to get news and research different topics. There are specific topics dedicated to the job search and if you are not utilizing this for recruiting you are missing out on some great advertising for your job (Example Below).

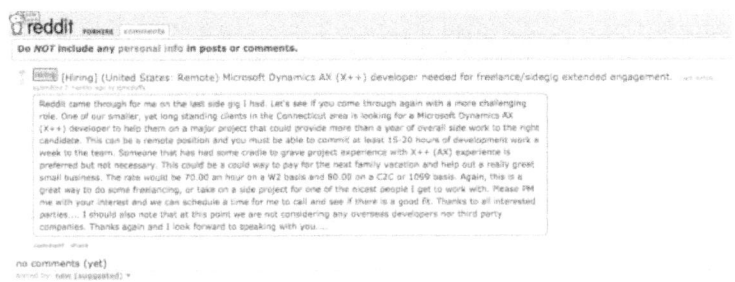

Use the Search bar to run a search

Reddit supports using Boolean Operators in search.

For example:

Search Javascript AND HTML "For Hire" Chicago

Or use Javascript AND HTML AND "For Hire" Chicago

Another example Javascript AND HTML ("For Hire" OR "available immediately" OR "Open to work" OR "looking for new opportunities") Houston

X-Ray search on Google

site:reddit.com/user "* * developer" "For Hire"

Searching for Remote Developers

site:reddit.com/user ("* Engineer" OR "* Developer" OR "* Programmer") "remote work" ("about me" OR "personal website")

Go where your candidates are and get to know the methods they are using to gain information. To get started with using Reddit for recruiting, here are some tips:

1. Know Your Platform

Before you jump into Reddit for recruiting, take some time to get to know the platform. If you have used it before, you are ahead of the game. Start by checking out subreddits like r/forhire to see what is currently being posted for roles. Reddit is different from other platforms you may use for posting jobs, so you will want to make sure you are using it properly.

If you are brand new to Reddit, start with the FAQ wiki to familiarize yourself with how to use it. Generally, you want your post to be upvoted so people see your post at the top and one that is vetting by other group members. You also want to get your Karma score high so Reddit users respect you. It is very different from LinkedIn or Facebook, so take the time to really learn how to use it for the best results.

Here's some Tech Subreddits:
DevOps Jobs: https://www.reddit.com/r/devopsjobs/
Java: https://www.reddit.com/r/java/
Front End: https://www.reddit.com/r/Frontend/
Learn Javascript: https://www.reddit.com/r/learnjavascript/

Here's some Diverse Subreddits:
Black Ladies: A safe place for Black women:
https://www.reddit.com/r/blackladies/
Native American: https://www.reddit.com/r/NativeAmerican/

2. Know Your Audience

Reddit is a fantastic place to recruit and source candidates for the tech industry. If you are looking for Programmers and Developers, they are very likely hanging out on Reddit. If your jobs are on this platform, you may get a more passive candidate that isn't' actively checking out traditional job posting sites.

84

There are certain protocols for recruiting on Reddit that you need to follow to avoid alienating the candidates you want to attract.

No spammy posts and super obvious advertising language. They will ask questions and expect you to have honest answers about the job.

3. Post Your Job

Every sub-reddit has specific guidelines, so the first step is to carefully read these and follow them. Don't assume the rules are the same for every sub-reddit you are using; you may find your post in the spam folder. In some cases, they may even ban you from participating in the future.

Formatting in Reddit is unique to the platform, so ensure you are doing this correctly. Check out Reddittext.com's guide for formatting to make sure your posts are on the right track. It's also a good practice to review the subreddit you are interested in posting to for examples of jobs that are highly upvoted by users with good karma ratings. See what they are doing and mirror their approach to get similar results.

4. Follow Up

Reddit is all about getting your questions answered, so you need to do this for your job as well. Posting and forgetting about it isn't going to provide you much return. People may ask questions directly in the sub-reddit or private message you.

Be available and actively participate in the sub-reddit you are posting in. This will help readers know, like, and trust you. Then they will give your job a more realistic look. If they feel like you are only there to promote your job and not help the community, they may be less likely to consider the opportunity. Workable mentions caring about your potential candidates goes a long way on Reddit and can help you achieve great results with recruiting.

Ensure you are honest in your answers, as Reddit users are no non-sense when it comes to being lied to. It's just good practice, to be honest about the job anyway. Candidates should come into a job knowing what to expect so that they can be successful.

If you aren't using Reddit as part of your Technical Recruiting strategy, it's time to check it out! Ere.com states that "Eighty percent of traffic comes from a desktop computer". This makes it great for candidates to check out your job and apply on the spot. Unlike other platforms that are usually viewed on mobile devices, where candidates either have to save a job for later or try to apply via their iPhone.

While using Reddit for recruiting is a bit more involved than posting to Monster, it can lead to fantastic results. For hard to source roles, like those in the Technology industry Reddit can aid in finding the best candidate for your role. Taking this approach will focus your extra energy on the roles that are difficult to fill. The best part? It is a free resource to market your jobs, so take advantage today!

Amazon Reviews Search

Amazon is the largest online shopping site. The site has roughly 12 million products to purchase, including Marketplace items that total goes to 350 Million available items to purchase.

"Our vision is to be earth's most customer-centric company; to build a place where people can come to find and discover anything they might want to buy online." This is Amazon's mission statement.

The number of available items and products is truly unbelievable. Amazon got started by selling books online. Why don't we use these great reviews to source and recruit potential candidates?

Amazon sells a ton of niche industry related books on any given topic. The shoppers that take the time to review a product are probably within that field of study. This idea is a creative way to find and reach out to potential leads. You can easily cross-reference someone's username and find them on other social media channels.

Here's how to search for Amazon Reviews:

Let's say you are searching for Software Engineers. Do a quick search on a book related to "Object Oriented Programming" Languages and start reading the book reviews.

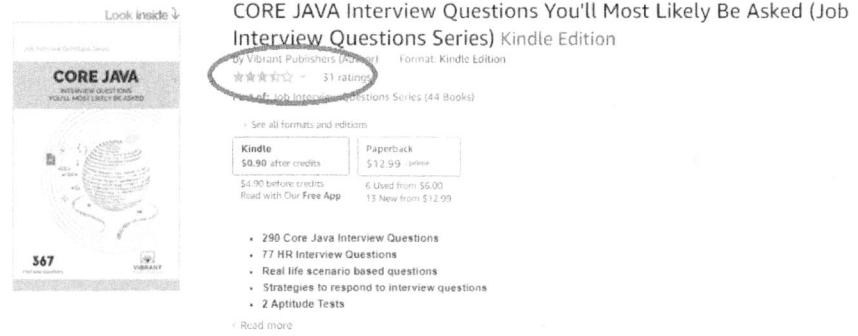

Read the reviews and search for the profile username info:

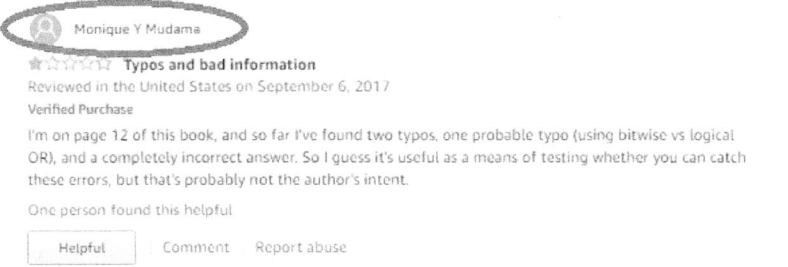

Conduct a quick Google search to find that user on social media. Bonus: SeekOut gives this candidates email address below.

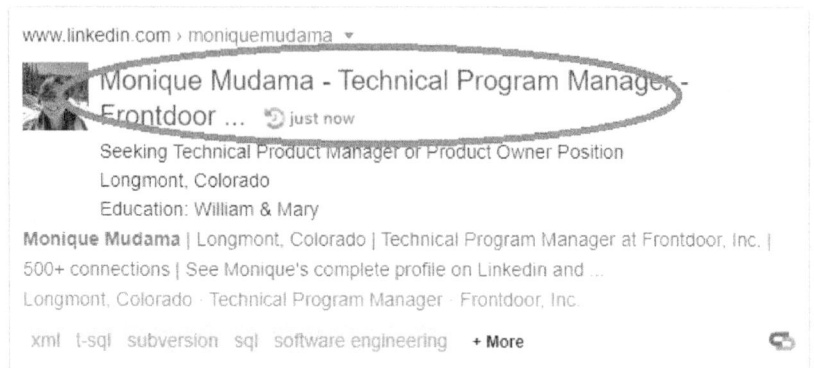

Finally, take all this information and write an email:

Hi (Name), I was doing a search on Java books on Amazon and came across your review. I was impressed by how you took the time to write a lengthy review on this topic. Great call out on the Typo issues. Looks like you're currently a Program Manager at Frontdoor. I wanted to see if you would be interested in learning about our (remote) teams at (company)

Quora Search

What if there was a site where you could find top industry professionals in different niche areas based on Q&A responses? It's a reality with the site Quora. With an estimated audience of over 700,000 it's also a spot to tap into some high quality talent. Recruiting in 2018 requires more than the typical tools and job board sites used traditionally. Posting roles on LinkedIn and Indeed are still a big part of finding top talent, but if you don't include new avenues, you are missing out on great candidates. Social media is an essential part of a successful recruiting strategy. One of the best ways to connect with candidates is by going to where they hang out. To help you add in a new source for talent, we have put together some helpful tips for you on recruiting on Quora.

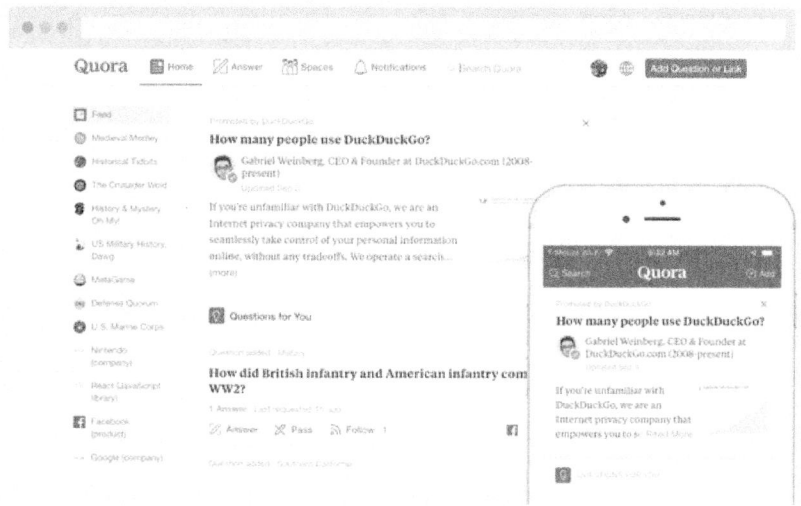

Provide Value

People are coming to Quora to find answers to their questions. Anything from 'what happens if I get fired' to 'help me with a coding issue'. Selling them on your job right out of the gate is likely not going to go over well. People will think you are using the site to push your own agenda versus what it is meant for. Instead, build trust with the users by being an active participant. Start by setting up your profile and let people know where you work and what you are qualified to answer questions on. Then locate the good forums to provide value in that will also get you seen by potential candidates. Search through the questions and see what you can answer. Another great option that Recruiter.com points out is to set up a company page so that users can learn about the company and provide positive reviews.

Locate the Experts

The best way to find the 'hard to find candidates' is to look to see who is answering the questions. Social Talent suggests searching for the keywords you need (think C++, Java, etc.) to see who is participating in the forums. These people are so skilled in these systems that they are helping others with it. These SME's are out there sharing their knowledge and making it easy for you to see they know what they are talking about. Instead of taking it at face value that they can use a certain system, you can see that they have by their answers to community questions. Once you find those candidates, reach out to them. Introduce yourself and see if they would be open to a quick conversation. Then you can informally talk to them about your company and gauge their interest in moving forward.

Time In and Results

Using Quora is not going to be a passive endeavor. You will need to commit to putting in the front end work to get the most return on your investment. When you show candidates that you are willing to help them with their recruitment questions, it will help you be seen as a recruiter they can trust. Participating in forums will set you apart from other recruiters than can be seen as just trying to fill a job.

Another great aspect to using Quora for recruiting is that the site provides you with analytics to see how you are doing. Just click on your profile picture and check out your stats. Seeing the views and up-votes you are generating will help you see if your efforts are paying off. Answering questions and getting up-votes will have a lasting long tail effect down the line when other users Google search for answers in the future. Industry professionals will connect your name with those answers and thus associate your name with other experts in the field.

Recruiting on Quora is a great addition to your recruiting strategy. People are using Quora to research all kinds of questions, including recruiting. You can show your expertise in your field to attract experts in the fields you are recruiting for. Get started today and gain access to candidates that you wouldn't have been able to reach before. Make 2018 the year you add social media to your search strategy and see some great results.

Stack Overflow Search

Are you having trouble finding qualified talent to submit to your technical job reqs? These candidates are not as engaged in typical sites like LinkedIn and don't apply to job openings on career sites as frequently. Because of their reclusiveness, it takes a bit of work to find them. To help yourself stand out as a recruiter and find talent that no one else has found, you have to be willing to think outside the box. If you are limiting yourself to standard candidate generation marketplaces like LinkedIn, you are missing out on potential talent that may be perfect for your role.

Stack OverFlow is a great option if you are looking to expand the net you are casting, particularly for technical candidates. So what is Stack OverFlow and how can you use it the source? This is exactly what we are covering in this article!

What Is Stack OverFlow?

Getting to the basics. If you aren't familiar with Stack OverFlow, you will need to know what it is before you start using it to find talent. To be honest, it reminds me of a super technical version of Quora. Basically it is a question and answer site for technical questions. Users can post questions, answer other user's questions, and upvote the answers on the site.

The types of people on this site are going to be programmers or those dealing with a programming language. If you are searching for an Investment Banker, this isn't the site for you. If you need a programmer, this is likely where they are hanging out. According to Social Talent, Stack OverFlow is the third-best platform for finding programmers.

Finding the Talent

91

There are two ways to search Stack OverFlow for candidates that have the skills you are seeking. There is the "All User Search" (aka free) and the paid Stack OverFlow careers site. Both are great options to locate the profiles of qualified developers.

All User Search – Stack OverFlow allows you to search profiles for profile information, in a roundabout way. The best way to search the platform is by using Google X-Ray. The main points of the profile you may want to include in your search string are location, and the tags they have contributed to. In many cases, the tags they are contributing to will give you information on the programming languages they are proficient in. According to some sites, X-Ray may not always work though. Check out Devskiller's in-depth article for more information on how to organically search the site.

Here's some Boolean string examples:

site:careers.stackoverflow.com "Java Developer"

site:stackoverflow.com/users "Java Developer"

site:stackoverflow.com/cv "* * developer|engineer" (c rust OR c++ rust)

Stack OverFlow Careers – They've created a specific site dedicated to career opportunities. With the paid option, you can directly post a role in this section to attract candidates using the site, search profiles, and set up a company profile page. Candidates interested in being found have the option to create a developer story. Those that you contact through this medium have a super high engagement rate, so if you can afford to put some money into it, this is a fantastic option. If your budget is nil, these profiles can be sources by using a search string on Google. It may take some trial and error to see which strings will give you the most desired results, but with some work, you can definitely find who you are looking for.

Browser Extensions Recommendations

- Search Stackoverflow: Easily find users and tags with this advanced searching tool.
- SeekOut: Great for finding user contact information.
- Hiretual: Great for finding user contact information.
- StackOverflow Power User: Find the best "power" users with this tool.
- StackEye: Get notifications about questions and from users in your watch-list.

Contacting Candidates

Once you find candidate details, the hardest part is engaging them. If you are still using standard copy and paste emails to your candidates, please end the madness! Particularly with developers and other difficult to find candidates. Their experience is in demand and due to that, they are being endlessly contacted. Showing you have no interest in them is a guaranteed way for your email to end up in the trash bin.

So how can you show your interest? Take the time to read through their profile. When you reach out to them, make a comment on something specific that you found out about them by doing your research. By doing this, you are letting them know you aren't just sending emails on mass, hoping to get someone hooked.

Make sure you have plenty of details on the role you are recruiting for as well. If you don't know what you are talking about, it will be difficult to convey to candidates that they may be interested in the role. These candidates are in demand, so if they don't get a good vibe from you, they know someone else will be contacting them soon.

Here's an example of a Recruiter Template:

Hi John, I was impressed by your recent answer to (post summary). I dove further into your profile and was again impressed by your high reputation score. I'm sure you receive a lot of fan mail but wanted to see if you would be open to learning about a new opportunity? (Job Link)

If you haven't started using Stack OverFlow as a part of your sourcing strategy, you are missing out on the third most successful site for sourcing developers. It will take a little work to find talent, but in this market it is necessary. Take some time to get familiar with the site and the methods we discussed in this article to stand out among your peers and fill that super difficult reqs.

GitHub Search

GitHub is the world's largest open-sourced repository coding sites online today. Currently, it has over 28 million users and over 57 million in repositories. With so many monthly active users sharing and learning about coding, it's a fantastic place for Talent Sourcers to find qualified talent. With the recent encouragement by Susanna Frazier, I wanted to reflect on GitHub and showcase how to source and recruit on this social network.

What's included in a user's profile?

Username – You can use this to crossreference on namechk.

Location – Another vital piece when sourcing.

Current Company – Another important piece.

Links – This includes contact information, websites, or blogs etc.

Number of Followers – The more followers means how skilled they actually are. Anything above 50+ is incredible.

Contributions – Use this to find additional keywords to search for.

Repositories – Review there open-sourced projects. Great place to share what they there currently working on.

Searching on GitHub

GitHub has two search engines one being a simple search and also an advanced search. Good to note, basic Boolean operators like AND, OR, NOT will work in searches. I've included some search parameters when searching directly in the search bar:

Language

Language:c++

language:javascript

Location

location:minneapolis

location:"minneapolis"

location:minneapolislocation:sanfranciscolocation:losangeles

Followers

followers:>5 -Searching users with more than 5 followers.

followers:<5 -Searching users with less than 5 followers.

followers:1..5 -Searching with users between 1-5 followers.

Username

author:example – searching for authored content.

user:example – searching in repositories.

created:2018 – looking to see when the user profile was created.

XrayingGithub

When xraying GitHub you should target both domains when searching: github.com and github.io. Also, I recommend searching through Google when doing these xray searches. I included some examples below:

Basic search

site:github.com "joined github" minneapolis "javascript"

Searching for Email Addresses

site:github.com "joined github" minneapolis "javascript" "*gmail.com"

Searching for the most active users

site:github.com "contributions in the last year" minneapolis "javascript"

Searching based on job titles

site:github.com "joined on" "public activity" -tab.activity "Java Developer" Minneapolis

Advice on Messaging Users

So, now you know how to search and Xray on GitHub. The tougher part is engaging and communicating with those users. GitHub is seen as a place to learn and not necessarily as a place to find a new job. Do not treat it like another LinkedIn resource. Here's some tips on communicating with users:

- Do not write in paragraph form. Use a few 2-3 sentences at most when reaching out.
- Focus on what they are working on. Try highlighting their recent project activities in the message.
- If they don't respond let it be. Do not over-communicate like on LinkedIn.
- I recommend (two outreaches) over GitHub directly and also over email.

Overall, I definitely recommend searching on GitHub. There's a ton of active monthly users that and might not even be active on LinkedIn. You need to use this resource as a way to expand on your searches when sourcing. Please let me know if you have any questions in the comment section below.

Slack Search

How many places do you use to recruit candidates? If you are only listing one or two places, it's time to add to your list. Recruiters need to look for various ways to find qualified candidates. We all know about using LinkedIn and other popular sites for sourcing, but what about something a little outside of the box?

Recruiters need to diversify the platforms they use to find talent because everyone else is using those same places. Have you considered the app Slack as a source for candidates? It is a hotspot for millennials and a place where you just may find your next superstar. If you are unfamiliar with Slack, we break it down for you and how you can use it for recruiting below.

What is Slack?

If you haven't heard of the app, it is a spot where people get together to talk about common areas of interests. The interests are grouped by communities and channels where people can talk with other members with the same interests.

Companies use it to communicate with teams quickly and individuals use it to talk about many different topics. The site is also indexed and every topic is saved and searchable. If you want a more detailed synopsis on what Slack is, check out their site here.

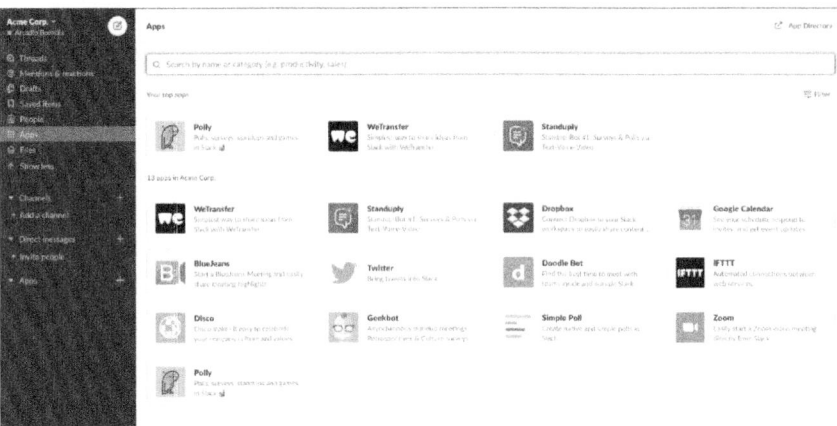

Why use it for Recruiting?

You will be where your candidates hang out. Instead of hoping they check their LinkedIn account once every two months, you can be sure they will be actively engaged. You can converse with people who are interested in the topics you are recruiting for. The site is also quick with people answering very fast to posts.

As I mentioned earlier, Slack is also searchable. If you are looking for a candidate with a specific skill set, you can search by that skillset to see what communities come up. You can then see who is active in the community and either post in the channel or send a direct message to those you are interested in.

Slack even has a page on how you can use the app for recruiting. Their page is all about how you can use it to keep everyone in the loop on the recruiting process. If you are a recruiter in a small company, this could be a great way to keep everyone up to date real-time.

How to use Slack for Recruiting

Check out the different communities to see which would be the best for the talent you are targeting. Here is a list of the top communities out there so you can start to see which ones would be worthwhile for your efforts. I've included my recommendations of communities to join below:

- Developer Communities
- Global Developers
- Front End Developers
- Ruby Developers
- iOS Developers
- Business Related Communities
- Latinx in Tech
- Women in Sales
- Black Engineers
- Startups
- Human Resource Communities
- HR
- Corporate Recruiters
- Career Related Communities
- Software Jobs
- Freelance Jobs

Pro Tip: Check out Slofile.com for a list of slack communities online. Once you've narrowed down the list use Phantombuster to pull a full list of users with emails if available.

Become active in the community by letting people in the group know you are a recruiter and what you are searching for. See who replies. Anyone who expresses an interest you should individually message and schedule some time to talk further. Just be careful that you are aware of the rules of the channel so you aren't doing anything that could be considered spam.

Start with getting yourself familiar with the platform, which you can so by reading tutorials and FAQs on the app. Then start researching different channels to target based on your candidate profile.

Once you identify the channels you want to be part of, start getting involved while following the Slack etiquette. Be careful with this especially on Slack because the people using the app are not necessarily interested in looking for new opportunities.

 Another option is to use Slack for employee referrals, as Workable points out. It's a quick and easy way for employees to let you know of candidates that they recommend. If you make it easy for employees to refer their peers then they are much more likely to actually participate, particularly if there is not a hiring bonus attached.

What Types of Candidates are on Slack?

The primary type of candidate on Slack are those with a technology focus. Startups and technology companies are using the app more and more to move away from the heavy reliance many companies have on email.

If you are in the IT recruiting space, I recommend you give Slack a try to have access to many candidates you may not have been able to otherwise contact. The IT industry is in high demand, and if a candidate is not actively looking for a new job, the chances of them being on LinkedIn or job board sites are pretty slim.

The world of recruiting is constantly changing. To be the best in your field, you must keep up with the changes in the market to continue to provide the best talent. You are on the right track with checking out this article!

Slack is still a new method to recruiting and one you could really capitalize on if you take the time to learn how to use it. It certainly won't be the last platform you will need to learn in your recruiting career, but you are still ahead of the game if you start now!

Meetup Groups

Meetup.com is an events based social networking site with roughly 30 million users, 300K groups, and 500K monthly meetups. Meetup can add incredible value when it comes to sourcing and recruiting talent across the globe. There's a lot of ways that you can search on Meetup.com for communities.

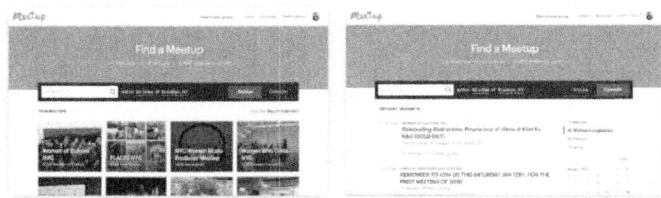

Profile Boolean string examples:

Here's all the different ways to source Meetup members and groups below. Remember to include diversity related terms within your search string.

Make sure to include searchable terms: ("Latino" OR "Spanish" OR "Mexican" OR "Latinx")

After a quick search I found this great group > NYC Latino Professionals - 4,400+ Members & Growing!

1. Member Search

site:meetup.com (java OR python OR ruby OR C# OR C++) "member since"

2. Member(s) Search

site:meetup.com/software/members/ (java OR python OR ruby OR C# OR C++)

3. Zip Code Search

site:meetup.com (java OR python OR ruby OR C# OR C++) 55110..554433 "member since"

4. Location State Search

site:meetup.com (java OR python OR ruby OR C# OR C++) intitle:"MN" "member since"

5. Location City Search

site:meetup.com (java OR python OR rubyOR C# OR C++) intitle:"minneapolis" "member since"

6. Network Search

site:meetup.com (java OR python OR rubyOR C# OR C++) "member since" "networks"

7. Groups events strings examples:

site:meetup.com "java" "meetups are scheduled"

site:meetup.com java intitle:MN meetups are scheduled

site:meetup.com "mobile" (kotlin OR android OR objective-c OR java) intitle:"minneapolis" "meetups are scheduled"

Note, since many pages have similar content I suggest using [-inurl:] to exclude certain pages from showing up. Make sure to play around with that search technique.

8. List string example:

Use these string below to find a list of Meetup's that match your search criteria:

site:meetup.com "minneapolis" intitle:software (intitle:"meetup groups" intitle:meetups)

Pro Tip: Check out Freesourcingtools.com custom CSE to search for events and groups.

Joining Groups

I recommend joining meetup groups within your search. You can try and directly message users from individual groups. Be as genuine and human as possible – some industries do not like talking with recruiters.

Attending Events

I recommend going to events on a quarterly basis! Build a network within your niche. Try and make yourself known in the local community.

Twitter Search

Twitter Search - Twitter's advanced search can help you to find people who are talking about a particular thing in a particular location - https://twitter.com/search-advanced

Twitter is a great resource to find active users within certain niches. You can easily find users that are active and posting within the tech world. More than ever, users are moving away from using LinkedIn. So, in some ways you will need to explore other social networks to find and engage talent online. I've included ways to source and recruit diverse talent on Twitter below.

Twitter's advanced search feature allows you to create complex searches that include both hashtags and keywords— so you can search for multiple criteria like job role, skillset, and location, along with URM or other identifying keywords. What's more, you can filter results by tweet, account, photo, video, and news.

Note that Twitter's advanced search only searches tweets; it won't pick up keywords in bios, where some of the best professional information (titles, skills, technologies) is found. You can get around this with a Google x-ray search: site:twitter.com ("solution architect" OR "solutions architect" OR "technical architect") lgbt -jobs –hiring.

Boolean Strings to Search Bios:

site:twitter.com inurl:with_replies [add keywords]

site:twitter.com "Tweets and replies" -inurl:with_replies [add keywords]

You can use Google Synatex to find certain users with the number of followers:

site:twitter.com "Tweets and replies" javascript engineer "200..1000 following"

Search for Hashtags:

#BlackTechTwitter

Finally, some Twitter diversity directories exist that have already done the work for you. Check out Blacks who Design, Women who Design, and Latinxs who Design, for example. You can filter down by role, and jump on a person's feed from there. They might not be a fit for the role you are working on, but connecting in these communities could lead you into other communities more targeted to your search.

Snapchat, Twitch, and Tiktok Search

The growing number of social media platforms has surely created a number of opportunities for recruiters. Of course, many are getting left behind because they're simply unsure of how to approach these brand new tools. If you feel the same way, this advice will help you out.

While not all tools are created equal, the likes of SnapChat, Twitch, and TikTok are among the most popular right now, and they also present many unique opportunities for your work as a recruiter. With companies looking to get costs – you may want to consider using free social networking sites to connect with candidates online.

In all honestly, I'm new to these platforms and I'm testing out each to see if they add value to my sourcing and employment branding strategies. It's good to go where the talent goes. So, if you see value in connecting with these users than it's worth creating a profile.

First Understand the Platforms:
Before you do anything with these platforms, the first thing you'll want to do is familiarize yourself with them a bit. This means creating an account and just spending some time seeing how others interact. Make sure that your target demographic is actively using these websites. This is perfect for targeting and sourcing GenZ and Millennials within your markets.

Snapchat
Is a platform to send instant view-able videos you can use humor and excitement to build an employerbrand.

Twitch
Is a live streaming platform created for gamers. Create a profile and connect with gamers across the globe. Many gamers are professionals in the tech community. You could use this platform to network and build a community of talent.

TikTok
Is a video sharing network. You can add comedic and fun videos on this platform. You can drive likes and engagement for your brand.

Each platform has its own unique style of content and you'll need to spend some time figuring out how you can best interact on each platform. Your approach will differ a bit between each one. I recommend doing research to see if you can gain value from using the platforms.

How to Use These Platforms:
Once you have a solid understanding of how each of these platforms functions, you can get to the fun part of actually posting content. Your goal, of course, is to use these platforms to promote a company's culture and open jobs, ultimately inspiring people to see the brand in a positive light, and perhaps even reach out if they're considering them as a potential employer.

The tricky part is figuring out what to post. You don't just want to plug a job constantly. Rather, you should take a step back and use these platforms as a method of taking people behind the scenes. Here are some ideas of what you can post:

1. Let Employees Take Over
Sometimes the best way to show off a company is to let someone from within the company present things in their own way.

Letting an employee "take over" one of your accounts for a day or more can give people a fun behind-the-scenes look at what goes on each day. For instance, maybe they'll walk people through their routine, which may include hitting up the company gym in the morning or playing with the office's beloved cat.

2. Share Live Virtual Events

Giving candidates exclusive access to live events the company hosts is another great source of content. Whether you're live streaming the coverage or sharing it after-the-fact, it can really help candidates get a closer look at what working with the company would be like. You can do these events virtually and share opportunities to a broader audience.

3. Go Behind-The-Scenes

Share a picture of that epic birthday party the team just threw for the new receptionist and maybe even give candidates a look into the development or collaboration processes that help the team thrive. It's this type of "behind-the-scenes" content that lets you pull back the curtain and really entice people to learn more and want to get involved. Share fun and exciting culture that highlights your employment brand well.

4. Build your Personal Brand

Recruiters need to build their personal brand online and it's good to get creative and stand above the crowd. If you are targeting members within these communities, it will make sense to invest in creating an account. Again, try and use humor to connect and engage with these users. The long term goal will be to build your brand and network with them.

While it will take some finesse in order to properly represent the company on each platform, adding these tools to your arsenal is surely worth it. Consider these platforms to be a top priority as you continue to build an employer brand that people want to interact with.

Chapter 5: Talent Sourcing Tools

Talent sourcing tools are important when it comes to finding and engaging talent online. There are many tools that focus on sourcing diverse talent. I wanted to highlight the top ones that most Recruiters and Sourcers recommend.

1. Native Current

This is a new tool that helps find diverse (BLNA) talent online. With the help of Boolean strings, it helps users find many diverse niche groups online. The helps Talent Sourcers uncover new talent BLNA pools. Native Current empowers Sourcers and Recruiters to creatively expand talent search to meet the demands of modern businesses. I recommend signing up for an account to learn more about all the tools amazing Boolean generator search features.

First, download and then sign up for an account:

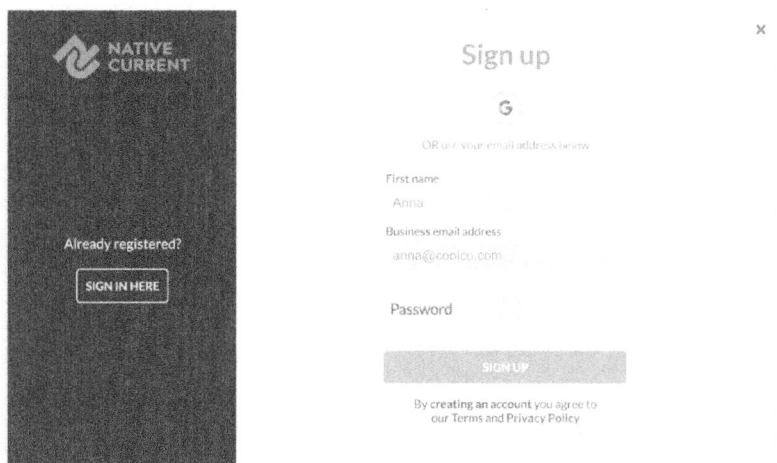

Second, type in the role that you are searching for:

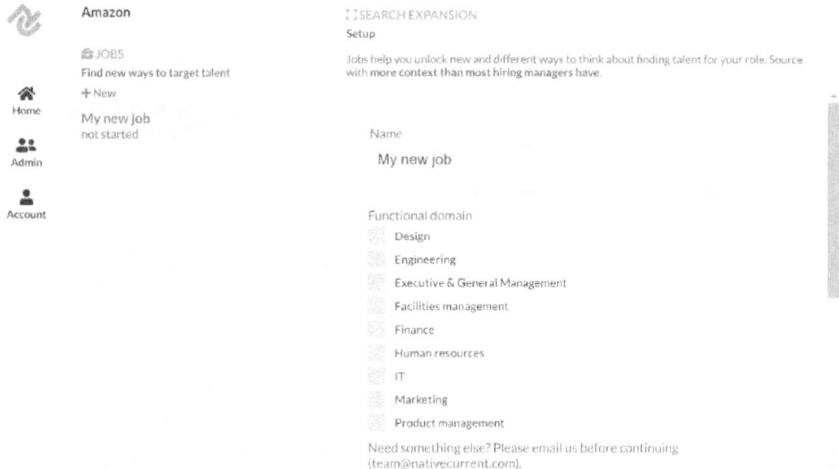

Select the diverse group that you want to find:

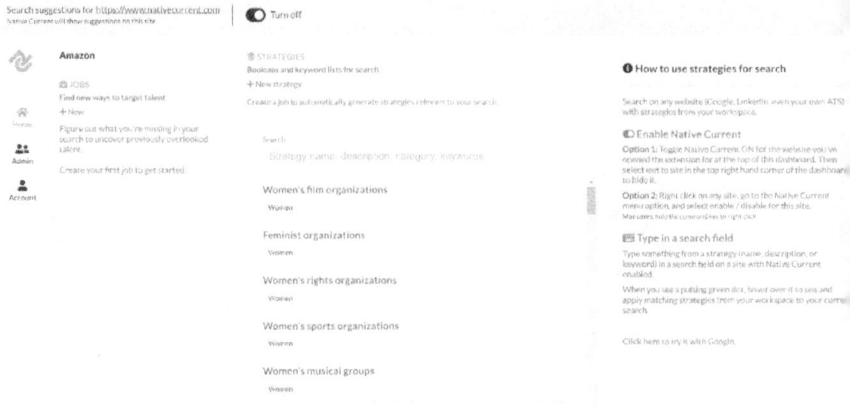

Finally, after you've selected the role requirement skills and diverse group. Then click open in Google.com

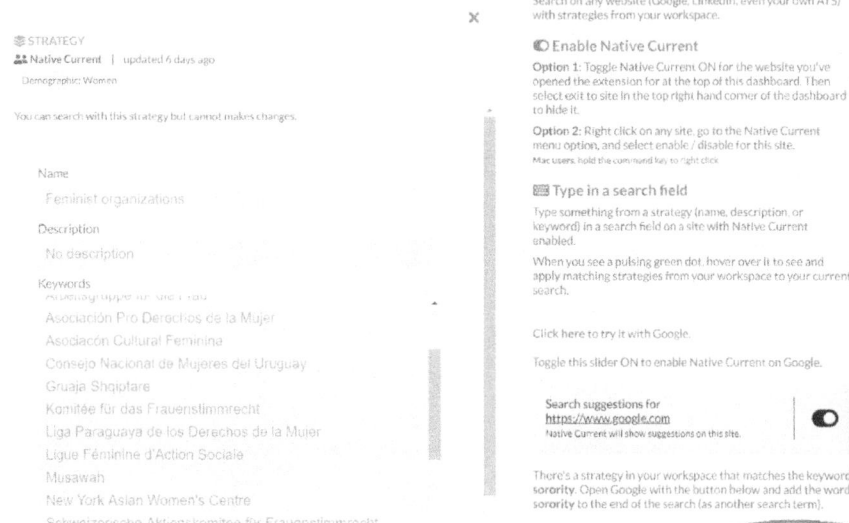

Search Features Include:

Enable Native Current:

Option 1: Toggle Native Current ON for the website you've opened the extension for at the top of this dashboard. Then select exit to site in the top right-hand corner of the dashboard to hide it.

Option 2: Right-click on any site, go to the Native Current menu option, and select enable / disable for this site.

Pro Tip: Enable the extension then type a job tile in LinkedIn Recruiter or Google the green button will appear and then you can choose a diversity Boolean string (Example Below).

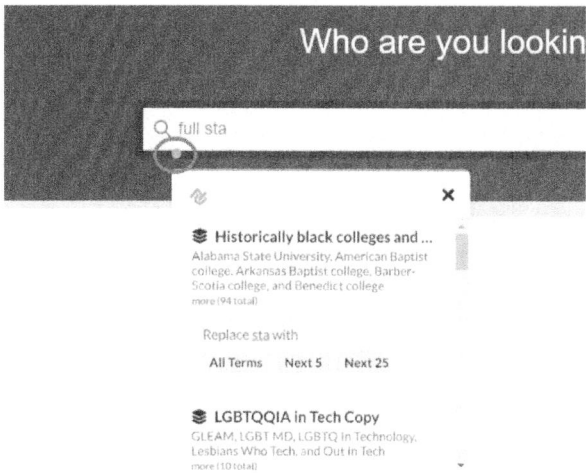

Native Current's Mission Statement:
We envision an American workforce characterized by equitable opportunity. One where diversity and opportunity are no longer at odds. Where businesses thrive in increasingly competitive markets because bringing people together has accelerated innovation and problem-solving.

A society where prosperity creates more opportunity for others, not less. We see sourcing enablement as a critical but overlooked step to creating a culture of opportunity in and outside of the workplace, and we're determined to break conventional ways of thinking about talent. No excuses.

1. Talent acquisition is more demanding than ever
Keep up with a platform that works everywhere you do, and gives your team a competitive advantage with the type of domain-specific insight only the best hiring managers have.

2. Run comprehensive searches anywhere
Search for talent on any website, and quickly apply relevant Boolean strategies without leaving the page.

3. Know what you're missing
Go beyond title-based searches with job expansion to automatically uncover and target new talent pools.

4. Search with precision confidently
X-ray social sites like Quora, Twitter, and LinkedIn with pre-built searches for your role.

Use the tool to search for diverse talent pools:

- **Women's Film Organizations**
- **Feminist Organizations**
- **Women's Right Organizations**
- **Hispanic and Latino American Organizations**
- **African-American Organizations**
- **LGBT QIA in Tech**

2. Human Predictions

Pair with this Bot to expand your candidate research.

We compile all the data for your potential candidates and automatically alert you about people we know information about. It's there when you need it and snoozes when you don't.

- Find people: Explore and find more about interesting people.
- Easily find diverse leads within this tool.
- Info at your fingertips: Get an email address and quick overview on anyone.
- Add data: Find a person/group you want to learn more about?
- You're in control: Hide it when you don't need it.

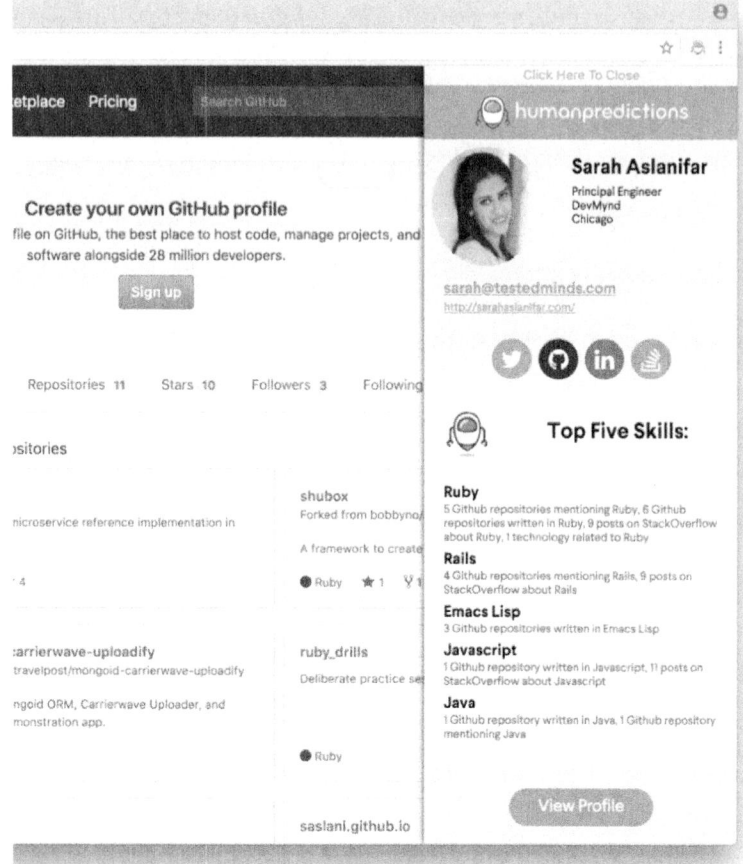

3. Entelo

This tool was founded in 2010 and, ever since, the software has been used by recruiters to proactively source diverse talent. It continues to be an industry leader thanks to its innovative diversity recruiting functions and many unique features. It will help you deliver the best candidates on the market.

It offers you the ability to find a diverse talent pool in mere minutes, focusing on under-represented groups by race, ethnicity, gender, and veteran status. You can also use it to eradicate your unconscious bias and quickly identify candidates that come from underrepresented groups thanks to the candidate badges that it lists on profiles.

It also allows your team to quickly track diverse leads throughout your process. Gain visibility into your organization's diversity, sourcing efforts and measure progress. Keep your talent team accountable by complying with federal regulations and demonstrating good faith diversity recruiting efforts.

You can select four major categories and also use them in combinations, e.g., Black AND Female. They also support filtering by various networks and groups.

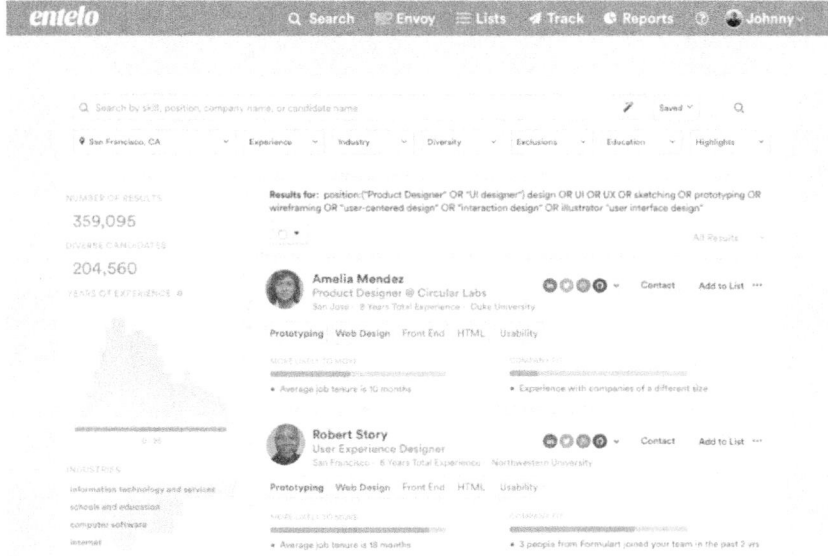

With Entelo go to the Settings, then Search and then choose Anonymize search results. Profile pictures are gone, and names turn to initials. This will help you search with unbiased results.

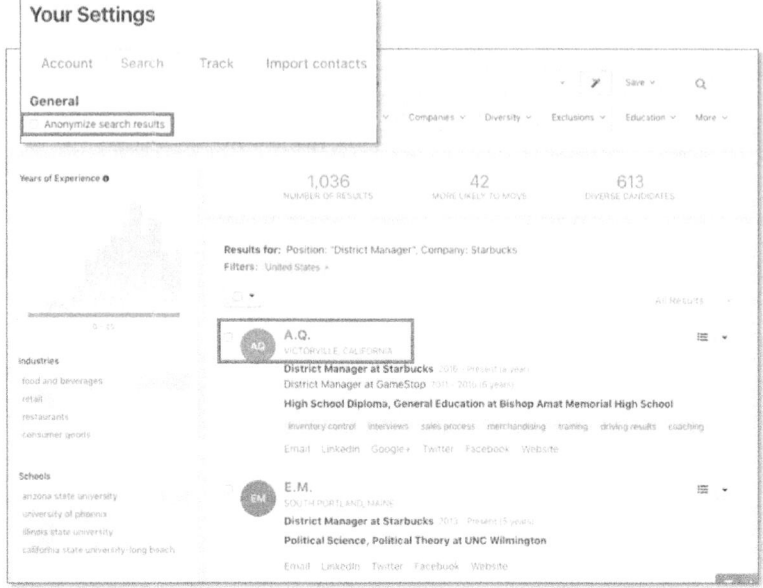

4. Hiretual

Hiretual claims to be the industry leader when it comes to AI-powdered talent sourcing, and they can certainly back that claim up with a wealth of features. Integrate Hiretual into your tech stack with ease and you'll instantly be able to source across over 750 million profiles.

One aspect you'll definitely appreciate about Hiretual is that it pulls information from over 40 platforms to build the single largest talent pool out there. Hiretual also goes a step further, helping you build powerful, personalized campaigns to engage top talent while actively rediscovering any profiles that are lost within your ATS.

Within their advance filters, you can search and find a list of diverse candidates. Now you can narrow your sourcing results to help widen the perspective of your organization. Specifically, Pro users can now filter sourced candidates to focus on women, veterans, African Americans, or Hispanics within your recruiting niche.

Rank and score the profiles that you are seeing to help Hiretual AI ranking search.

Use Hiretual's Talent Insights feature to search for diverse groups based on location, job title, or industry,

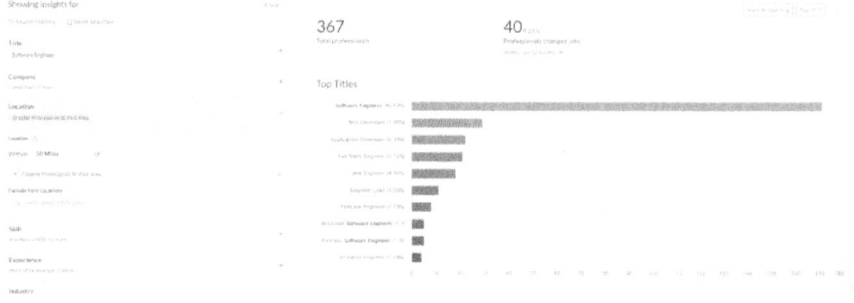

5. Seekout

Known for being extremely recruiter-friendly, Seekout is a platform that allows you to easily source passive candidates with the help of diversity filters. Other features, like getting contact info in just one click, also help Seekout stand out from the crowd. With a 360-degree view of the talent, Seekout provides a rich database like no other. The Ai-powered Seekout Robot also helps you get to the right talent as quickly as possible.

You can select major categories of diversity, and see filtered results with one click. One aspect that stood out for me was that SeekOut shows how many profiles correspond to a diversity category in advance of the recruiter applying that filter.

Verified emails and social profiles are available at the click of a button and you can send personalized automated emails to reach out to candidates with ease. You'll find that the diversity filters are especially helpful for finding female, Hispanic, African American, and Veteran candidates. This tool has so many other advanced features – I strongly recommend doing a demo.

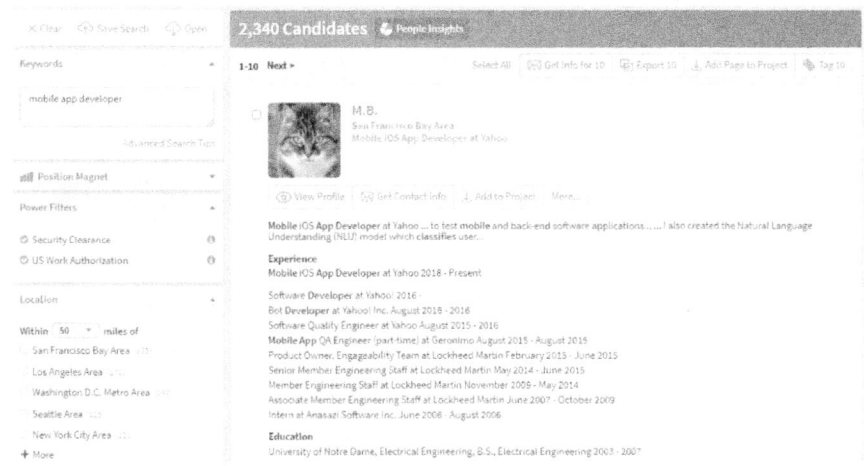

To reduce bias, select Blind Hiring Mode. All profile pictures turn to the same cat image (no bias from people's cat preferences) and names to just initials.

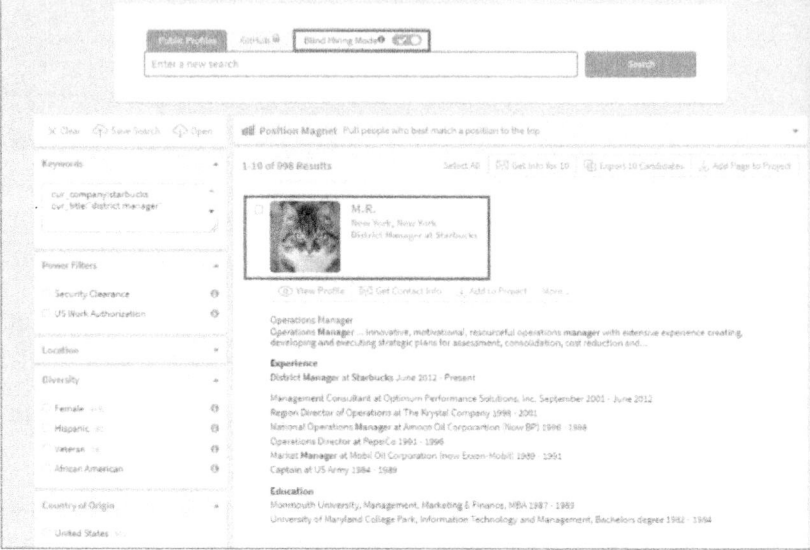

6. Diversifytech.co - Looking to build a diverse pool of candidates in the tech space? The simplicity and openness of Diversifytech.co leaves nothing to be desired. This site quite literally acts as a job board with information about candidates readily available to anyone looking to hire. You can search for candidate talent within this community. Overall, I highly recommend using this free resource when it comes to sourcing tech talent.

A collection of resources for underrepresented people in tech

Once a week, we'll send you scholarships, events, job opportunities, and more.

Subscribe

Hiring? Click here ...

7. JopWell is a community platform to help find diverse candidates for career opportunities. They support Black, Latin X, and Native American students and professionals across North America.

The focus on candidates who are underrepresented in the tech space, so it's a great additional source to check next time you're looking for candidates to reach out to in order to hit the mark regarding the number of diverse leads you're looking to engage.

8. Unbiased Search Extension - Use this to turn everyone's photo into a picture of a dog. This will help you to search for profiles based on keyword terms and not on race/gender.

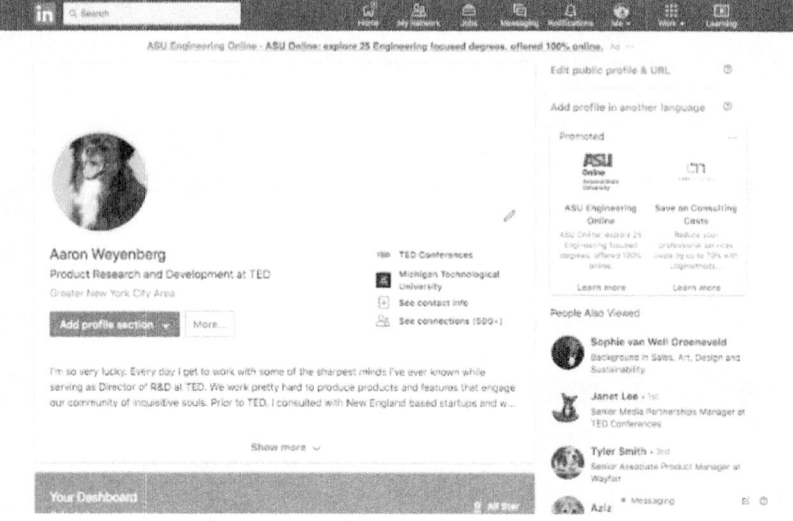

9. Tineye - use this tool to reverse search images online. You can search for profile images or other social media pictures within this tool.

Pro tip: You should try and reverse image search someone's headshot profile on other websites to build a larger view of someone's skill-sets.

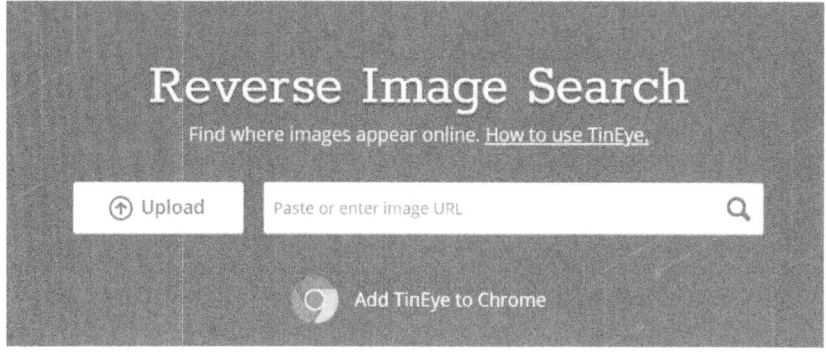

10. Yandex – as another great example to reverse image search online. You can search for images, videos, and much more.

Images   Video   Mail   Maps   AppMetrica   Translate   Browser

Yandex   Search

Automation Tool Suggestions

Recruiters spend the majority of the day sourcing and conducting research. There's a ton of great tools that automate many mundane tasks. There are many other automation tools that I could suggest but wanted to focus on the core ones that are highly beneficial.

Phantombuster

Rating: Beginner

Features:

- Extract data from platforms
- Profile scraper, social media scheduler, Auto responder and much more
- Automate repetitive tasks with talent sourcing
- Combine with AI to save more time

Phantombuster is used to extract data from platforms that can be used to automate necessary but repetitive tasks in recruiting. Phantombuster can be programmed to search certain profile data or URLs across networks such as Instagram, LinkedIn, Facebook, and Twitter, which can be compiled into a spreadsheet or CRM for review. The collected data can also help generate leads, be used to update network profiles, and be shared with others.

AI and other automation tools have definitely been on the rise lately. It's an exciting time to be in the talent sourcing world because we can use these same cutting-edge innovation tools to source, research, and automate certain recruitment tasks.

It was created to help marketers use different API's to automate and boost different marketing efforts. You can use one API tool for 10 minutes a day for free. I recommend testing out several tools before you decide to pay for the upgraded growth hacker account – which is $29 per month.

Tool Recommendations:
- Facebook Profile URL Finder
- Instagram Profile URL Finder
- LinkedIn Profile Scraper
- Twitter Profile URL Finder
- LinkedIn Accept Invitations
- LinkedIn Network Booster
- LinkedIn Search Export
- LinkedIn Auto-Follow/Accept

IFTTT
Rating: Beginner
Features:
- Easy-to-use automation tool
- Connects with all sorts of apps
- Create your own "recipes" to reduce your workload

IFTTT stands for 'If This Then That,' and is an ideal tool for email automation. With features that allow you to create reminders for yourself, handle repetitive tasks, and formulate specific triggers. It's a free, web-based service to create chains of simple conditional statements, called (applets) recipes.

These recipes help to automate different tasks. You can use these recipes to automate different recruitment activities. I encourage you to play around with these different recipes and figure out which ones work best for your needs. These tools will truly impact the way you automate certain recruitment and talent sourcing duties.

The user-friendly application requires a brief setup to connect the various platforms used including LinkedIn, Dropbox, Google calendar, and Facebook, to program the desired actions.

Some useful actions might include sending an email to yourself when new jobs are posted on LinkedIn or Craigslist; programming your phone to automatically text you, providing an escape for those times when an interviewee has exceeded their block of time, and you can't get away. I wrote an article about the best IFTTT recipes for recruiting here.

Recipe Recommendations:

1. New LinkedIn contacts in a Google Drive Spreadsheet
2. Send new contacts a "Nice to meet you!" email
3. Save contacts added to a Google Contacts group as a subscriber to a list in MailChimp
4. Save caller's contact info each time I receive a call
5. Create a calendar item to follow-up in a week when a new contact is added

Zapier
Rating: Intermediate
Features:
- Integrate multiple web apps

- Create custom automations
- Connect with over 1,500 platforms

Zapier is an application that makes it possible to integrate various other web based apps as a way to customize the automation. Zapier can communicate with other platforms including Office 365, Google Calendar, Google Docs, Gmail, QuickBooks, Trello, Airtable, Slack, and LinkedIn. Through the use of Zapier, you can share information between multiple apps automatically versus repeat manual entry. Zapier can help streamline the process of sorting and selecting candidates based on criteria, so you have more time to focus on evaluating information or actually connecting with candidates.

I discovered Zapier a few months ago and I've been hooked ever since! It's similar to the website IFTTT where I've been experimenting with recipes for many years now. However, Zapier is a way better automation tool in comparison. Zapier is the glue that connects over 1,500+ web apps. These apps connect together to trigger an event. You can use these pre-built zaps to automate mundane recruitment tasks. These apps can help with Calendar Scheduling, Call Tracking, Contacts, CRM, Emailing, Management tools, Human Resource tools — and the lists goes on! There are endless opportunities to use these apps in recruitment.

Zapier App Recommendations:
- Create Google Calendar events (quick add events) from Evernote reminders.
- Update rows on Google Sheets when someone new cancels on Calendly.
- Create Google Sheets rows from scheduled Calendly events.

- Create a call log or meeting note in Streak when a Calendly event is created.
- Send emails to lost Myphoner leads via Gmail.
- Send emails to new Myphoner winners via Gmail.
- Enrich company names in Google Sheets with data from Clearbit.
- Add person and company data from Clearbit to new MailChimp subscribers.
- Search Clearbit and save the results to Evernote via a Google Chrome extension.
- Enrich contacts in Google Sheets with emails and phone numbers using Lusha.
- Enrich new contacts on HubSpot CRM with enhanced personal contact details via Lusha.
- Create or update HubSpot CRM contacts from new Google Contacts.
- Create Streak boxes for new Google Contacts.
- Create boxes in Streak from new updated rows in Google Sheets.
- Save new Gmail attachments (original file format) to Google Drive.
- Look up a Google Sheet row and find & edit a box in Streak from new Gmail threads.
- Create a MailChimp Mailing List for Job Applicants.
- Import Job Candidates from Gmail into Workable by Labeling Emails.
- Create Workable candidates from a Google Sheets spreadsheet.

Airtable

Rating: Intermediate

Features:

- Easily link related data records
- Use Blocks to visualize and summarize

- Utilize pre-built templates
- Create your own templates and integrate with other tools
- Easily create a sales tracker, sourcing funnel, or ATS/CRM system

Use this tool to create a highly personalized ATS/CRM for tracking diverse leads.

Airtable combines the best features of database applications and spreadsheets into a single 'hybrid' application that allows you to compile information, sort data, link items together, share the information with others, and publish details on websites.

Its ability to integrate with applications such as Zapier makes it possible for recruiters to track candidates and share pertinent information via email. It's a great option if you are looking for a personal application tracking system or CRM tracker.

Airtable can also be set up to include candidate overviews and shareable links to their complete profile and credentials, enabling hiring managers to review specifics.

Template Recommendations:
1. Applicant tracking system (ATS) template
2. BLNA Tracking template
3. Employee Onboarding Template
4. University Recruiting or Job Fair event list Template
5. Competitor Tracking Template
6. Email Marketing Campaign Template

Chapter 6: Best Practices for Sending Messages

Crafting a perfect recruiter message takes time. In order to engage and get a response from a diverse lead you will need to understand the fundamentals of creating and creating an email or inmail message. Below I will walk you through examples.

Note: These examples would work best in North American markets only. The European market is quite different when it comes to messaging candidates online.

Looking to write the perfect recruiting cold call email? There are six elements you should consider critical when writing an email to a passive candidate. Recruiters need to spend the time to craft a message that is unique and personalized for reach lead. You will only have a few seconds before that lead is either responding or sending your email to the trash bin.

1. The Subject Line

Keep your subject line under 30-40 characters to make sure mobile users can read it. Remember, your subject line determines whether or not your prospect will actually open and read your message. Try to appeal to their ego and you'll give them a "mini high" that will have them wanting more.

2. Paragraph I

The first "paragraph" should really only be a few sentences long. You should warm them up by starting off with an explanation of how you reached out to them specifically with this role in mind. Tell them how you found them, too. You should be working to prove that you did your homework. Share there blog, portfolio, social media profiles within this first paragraph. Try and pull them in with your interest.

3. Paragraph II

In the second paragraph, you need to tell the prospect what they want to know about the role you're offering up. They mainly want to hear about a career trajectory, the expectations of the role, and the responsibilities they'd be taking on. Be honest about the workload and walk them through a "day in the life" in this position. According to LinkedIn, this is what candidates want to know the most. They want to under the project or team and what they are trying to accomplish.

4. Paragraph III

In your third paragraph, you should touch on your Employee Value Proposition, or EVP. That means covering the unique benefits the prospect would get to enjoy as an employee of your company. Make sure you frame these benefits as perks that they'll get in exchange for bringing their unique skills and experience to the company, that way you continue to make them feel good about what they have to offer.

EVP might include discussing how there are no product managers, meaning they'll get to drive the product development from beginning to end. You might also point out all the growth opportunities they'll have in front of them as you expand your team to double or triple in size in the next year. Talk about the flexibility of the environment and other things they'll enjoy. An example for us is that we've gone fully remote – that's a huge plus for candidates during this time.

5. The Call to Action

Your call-to-action, or CTA, is all about getting your prospect on the phone. If you can do that, you've achieved your goal. Your CTA should be short and friendly, just like the rest of your email. Some people employ the strategy of telling the prospect when they'll call, like saying: "I'll try to catch you on the phone this Friday at noon" or you can take a more traditional approach and offer them to connect.

Be sure to keep your CTA cool and casual. This is a friendly conversation, not a sales pitch–or, at least, that's how it should feel. Using humor has help me to get leads to respond: sending a meme or picture of my dog has paid off many times. The point is try and use creative ways to force them to respond.

6. The Signature

Your signature is critical because that's where your prospect will look to find your contact info and anything else they need to know to get in touch with you. Then leave your number as well. This is how they'll be able to reach out to you now that your cold call email has sold them on the idea. I like to bold my cell number and include my time zone.

7. Personalization & Uniqueness Get Responses

Whenever reaching out to a candidate, be personalized and avoid using generic templates. Take the job out of the conversation; do not start the message or email by saying you have an opportunity. Always start the message mentioning something specific about the candidate and what made you want to reach out? Having 10 people respond from 20 reach out messages if far more efficient than sending out 100 messages and still only 10 responses.

Whenever reaching out to candidates keep the following in mind:

- Unique & Creative subject lines!
- Personalized Content
- Aim for > 50% response rate
- Keep the word count to under 500 characters
- Is your message optimized for reading it on a mobile device?
- Keep sentences short
- Free of spelling & grammatical errors (Download and use Grammarly)
- Include questions and call for action

131

- The LARGER the volume per batch of reach outs, the LOWER the response rate
- Never let a response go to waste, set up future touch points
- Meme's, gifs, pictures, or emoji's work to cause a positive reaction

The right subject line is the secret to an effective recruiting email, so why do most people spend just mere seconds writing one when they can spend an hour or more creating the email itself? If you're doing things right, you'll spend at least as much time considering your subject line as you do your email's content because, after all, if the subject line isn't an attention-grabber, the rest of the email will never be seen anyway.

Of course, it can be tough to come up with a succinct and engaging subject line, especially for recruiting emails. To help you out, here are some ideas you can use, ranging from funny to those that provoke curiosity or a fear of missing out (FOMO) so that you can get more opens and, ultimately, more responses.

Here's the Best Recruiting Email Subject Lines I have found online:

Make Them Laugh

A clever subject line can certainly grab a candidate's attention. Take these, for example...

- Seeking a Tiger King Carole Baskin need not Apply
- I tried calling earlier but got crickets
- Re:re:re:re:re:re:re:My Last Follow Up
- We're Still Hiring During the Apocalypse

Provoke FOMO

"Fear of Missing Out" comes from a candidate realizing how great an opportunity is. These subject lines help provoke this sensation…

- Matthew, I'm Building An Avengers Marketing Team
- This Job Is Better Than a Friday Night at [Popular Bar Near Prospect's College]
- Let me introduce you to a better opportunity, Matthew.
- How's 2020 Starting at [Company]?
- We have Zoom Parties on Fridays

Entice Curiosity

Get them thinking about a position's potential with one of these enticing subject line examples…

- Matthew, Picture Yourself Creating [product] at [company name]
- Have you heard about [company name]'s upcoming launch?
- Your resume caught my interest, Matthew!
- Who's the worst boss you ever worked for, Matthew?
- What's the best job you ever had, Matthew?

Be Friendly in your Follow-Up

Follow-up requires unique personalization to spark a conversation. Take a look at these examples.

- How's your job at [current company] going?
- Can we talk about your boring job, Matthew?
- Let's have a convo about your future
- Want to grab a coffee with me next week?
- Do you have time for a chat about your career?
- I Just Left you a Voicemail

Dealing with a Crisis

What are their current needs? What are their current circumstances? Are your prospects stuck at home? Are they dealing with taking care of their children or finding ways to continue their education during quarantine? Are they trying to provide for family members at high risk? It's good to factor in these thoughts into your subject line when reaching out to passive applicants.

- Matthew, I'm just checking in with you
- How's work been at [company]?
- We're GROWING under uncertainty

Best Practices

As you read through these examples and search for inspiration to craft your own recruiting subject lines, don't forget about the best practices surrounding writing the best subject lines.

In general, the most engaging subject lines are between 61 and 70 characters long. You should tweak your subject line until you get it to this range, always remembering to keep things succinct. Every word counts in such a short string of letters, so come up with multiple versions and pick the one you think gets your point across best.

Remember, your subject line is only the introduction to your email. You don't have to say it all in the subject line, and there's no way you could. Rather, try to get the most important idea across in your subject line so that the person actually cares to open up the email and see what it's all about.

Finally, make sure that your subject line ties into the rest of the email. The first one or two lines of the email need to capture their attention just like the subject line did in order to pull them in so they read the whole thing. Your subject line should be relevant to what you're saying in the email–no click baiting!

Chapter 7: Employer Branding Tools

Employment branding is so important when trying to attract diverse applicants. You will need to market your brand online using marketing tools. By representing your brand by sharing content, videos, and pictures of your diverse team, you will attract a better pool of talent.

Applicants will research a company before they even consider applying for a job opening. Having content online that showcases your employer brand will be important.

Use video to send personalized videos to candidates. It's a new creative way to reach and engage a new audience.

LinkedIn Video

Recording a video can be a great medium to attract and engage potential lead when recruiting them. When you tailor a message specifically for someone odds are they will view and respond back to your message. Maybe you didn't realize this but you can now send video messages over LinkedIn messenger using their iPhone or Android app for free.

Why Send a Video at All?

A video is a great way to quickly tailor a message to your lead. On average, adding a video into an inmail or email will increase a response by almost 80%. On LinkedIn, they say that on average responses will increase by 50% when a recruiter shares a video in the inmail message. The fact is people love viewing pictures, memes, or videos more than reading long messages.

How to Send a Video Message on LinkedIn

The first step will be to send a connection request to the profile. Once they accept you'll be able to send a personalized video message using the LinkedIn app simply go into the messaging function of the app and click on the (+) to create a video message.

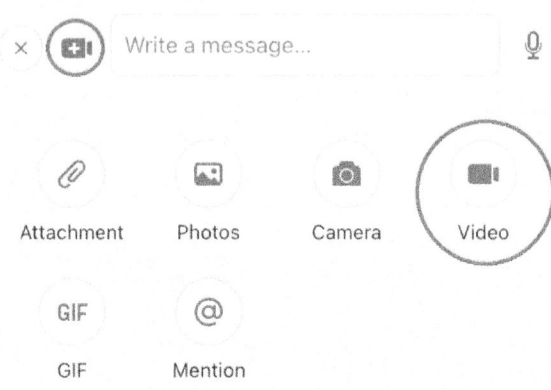

Tip: You need to be connected with the person before you can send them a video message.

I recommend recording a video no longer than 60 seconds. Be direct and focus on why you want to connect with that lead. Make sure you are in a quiet and well lit room with no background clutter. State the reason for the connection and why you would like to connect them. Once you send the message, allow them a few days to respond and then follow up. A concise video message will help convey that you value their time and will let them know why you want to connect with them.

SendSpark Extension (Desktop Option)

Let's say you don't have access to downloading the LinkedIn app. No problem, there is an extension called SendSpark that will allow you to create a quick video and send it directly over LinkedIn on your desktop computer. They have features to help track and review metrics after you send the message. Overall, it's a great tool if you want to invest in video messaging.

MyRobotWorks Extension (Desktop)

This extension allows you to attach video files when you auto send out messages on LinkedIn (desktop). Once you attach and send the message, it will autoplay the video message on LinkedIn.

Live Stream Events

Within the app or desktop LinkedIn, you can also live stream events. The LinkedIn Live feature allows individuals and organizations to broadcast live video content to their network in real-time. To get started, you can apply to become a LinkedIn Live broadcaster by completing an application.

This is a great avenue if you are hosting virtual career fairs or presentations. You can highlight what your team is working on and get instant access to responses and viewership. The ideas are really endless when it comes to live streaming.

Overall, video messaging is here to stay in the recruiting space! It's a fun and creative medium to reach out to potential leads and distinguish you from your competition.

Boomboom Video
This tool is a simple yet useful tool that delivers a personalized video message to each potential lead. The job market is very competitive at the moment. Job seekers are bombarded with potential opportunities by recruiters nonstop. So, that's why it's even more important to personalize every message when you can during your initial outreach.

What this tool offers:

1. Send simple video. There is no faster way to record, send, and track video. Within the dashboard, you can quickly record a personalized video and send it over email or text message.

2. Sales platform – you can create different lead forms and automate different email follow up. It's a fairly easy dashboard to understand.

3. Once the video is sent, you can easily track all the analytics. How long did the person view it? Use this Intel to improve your overall messages.

4. Pricing is billed at a yearly price at $468 which includes over 2,500 outreach contacts.

Social Media Tools:
These tools help you fully automate your social media presence online. In order to stay trending, you need to promote content on a weekly basis. This can become tiresome and take a lot of time, but thankfully we have tools that help automate these tasks altogether.

Sprout Social: Social management and marketing to customer care, employee advocacy, data metrics, and intelligence. It's an all in one tool that helps monitor and creates engagement over social media.

Hootsuite: Schedule social media content, curate from content libraries, and monitor conversations about your brand and your competition online.

Buffer: Schedule and curate content. This tool is great for larger teams looking to build out a large content calendar for employment branding campaigns.

Chapter 8: Job Description Tools

A clear, compelling, and inclusive job description will influence the candidate's decision to apply for the role and help cast a wide net to bring in the best applicants from many diverse backgrounds.

Applicants are looking for the following (4) factors before they consider applying:

1. A clear understanding of the company culture.
2. Insight into the employee experience.
3. A sense of connection with the overall brand.
4. What will this project or team be working on?

Start with what the candidate will do in the role: The first 90 characters are the most important, because it will set your role apart from others on the search results page.

Outline the essential functions and responsibilities as well as information about how the role will work with other teams if applicable.

1. **Basic qualifications:** are the minimum qualifications that an applicant must possess to be considered.

2. **Preferred qualifications:** are core competencies, subjective requests, or soft skills that can't be determined from the resume alone

Make sure to include mandatory EEO and Compliance Taglines for US based roles.

For example:
"(Company) is an equal opportunity employer and does not discriminate on the basis of race, ethnicity, gender, gender identity, sexual orientation, protected veteran status, disability, age, or other legally protected status."

In order to gain applicants, you will need to make sure your job descriptions are fully optimized. There are many terms that negatively impact a description. Make sure you are using gender neutral terms and words that do not relate to gender or race.

There's many tools available online that can help with optimizing your job descriptions.

1. Text Analyzer

The Text Analyzer is a basic augmented writing tool that's specifically made for job-related content. The tool was created to eliminate bore and bias. It will analyze your descriptions in real time to find gender and non-gender bias while also optimizing the length and title of your description.

This tool will also highlight parts where you overuse bullet points or adverbs, plus flag text that could lead to applicants not applying to your openings.

Are you writing job descriptions that are too "clinical" or "legal-sounding"?

- Job titles – Are yours optimized for apply rate and search engine optimization?
- Are you worried that some of your job descriptions are too long?
- Do you confuse your candidates with inside jargon (acronyms or department/business unit names)?

2. Textio

Textio is made for a number of uses, and one of the most popular is to help employees find better words to attract the right people. It will predict how the things you write will help you attract talent and make suggestions to help you find better qualified and more diverse candidates.

Ultimately, it will cut down the time you spend writing and the Textio Score will help you predict how well the description will perform in the current job market.

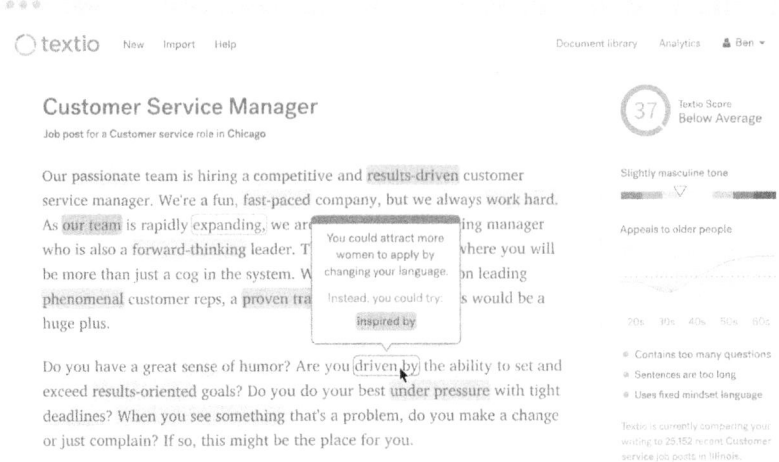

3. TapRecruit

The TapRecruit Smart Editor is a software focused specifically on augmented writing for job postings. The Smart Editor's goal is to help recruiters like you produce more thoughtful and concise job descriptions that will welcome a diverse range of candidates.

This tool will also provide a score for your job description, which will be based on the title, structure, and language that may leave a potentially bad impression.

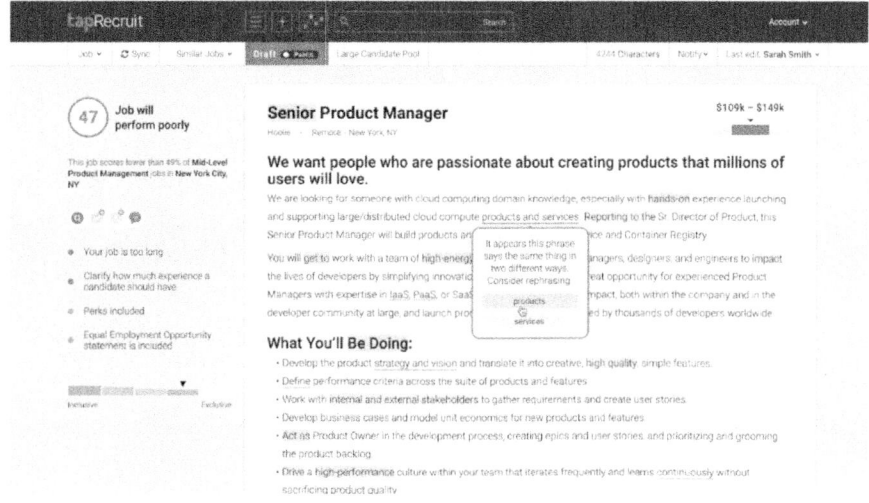

4. TalVista

TalVista offers a tool called Job Descriptions Optimized. This augmented writing software uses algorithms to help recruiters like you create more effective descriptions for your job postings, and it includes real-time feedback on what you write.

This tool will analyze the job description and identify problematic words, based on research, that have been shown to detract under represented applicants from applying for a job. The platform goes beyond gender parity, compared to others on the market, to ensure the broadest and most diverse applicant pool is attracted to the job.

Features include flagging of problematic words and phrases along with suggesting replacements that are more inclusive. It also provides a job score based on the best practices TalVista has created.

Identify problematic terms and replace with inclusive terms for:

- Gender Parity

143

- People of Color
- People with Disabilities

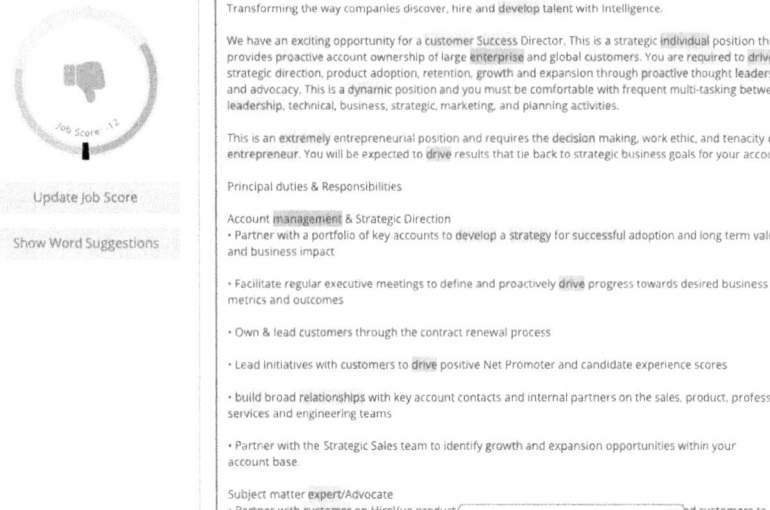

Transforming the way companies discover, hire and develop talent with Intelligence.

We have an exciting opportunity for a Customer Success Director. This is a strategic individual position that provides proactive account ownership of large enterprise and global customers. You are required to drive strategic direction, product adoption, retention, growth and expansion through proactive thought leadership and advocacy. This is a dynamic position and you must be comfortable with frequent multi-tasking between leadership, technical, business, strategic, marketing, and planning activities.

This is an extremely entrepreneurial position and requires the decision making, work ethic, and tenacity of an entrepreneur. You will be expected to drive results that tie back to strategic business goals for your accounts.

Principal duties & Responsibilities

Account management & Strategic Direction
• Partner with a portfolio of key accounts to develop a strategy for successful adoption and long term value and business impact

• Facilitate regular executive meetings to define and proactively drive progress towards desired business metrics and outcomes

• Own & lead customers through the contract renewal process

• Lead initiatives with customers to drive positive Net Promoter and candidate experience scores

• build broad relationships with key account contacts and internal partners on the sales, product, professional services and engineering teams

• Partner with the Strategic Sales team to identify growth and expansion opportunities within your account base.

Subject matter expert/Advocate
• Partner with customer on HireVue product   Thorough Deep Meaningful Excellent ad customers to effectively integrate digital interviewing into

• Advocate for customers internally helping build and maintain Strong partnerships with the sales, product administration and marketing teams

Update Job Score

Show Word Suggestions

5. BeApplied

This tool helps you detect gender bias in your job postings. It will identify any language that is gendered and give you an inclusion score so that you can better predict how your job description will be perceived by a broader audience.

The conversion score will then go over factors like readability and fluency, helping you note how easy it is to understand the job posting. The Applied JD Analysis Tool is pricy, but it's also highly effective.

Detect problematic phrases Acronyms, buzzwords and overemphasis on education.

These are just some examples that can introduce ambiguity, signal belonging (or not) and exclude people who are older, younger or from different socioeconomic backgrounds. The JD analysis tool highlights any instances of bias to give you the best chance of converting talented candidates.

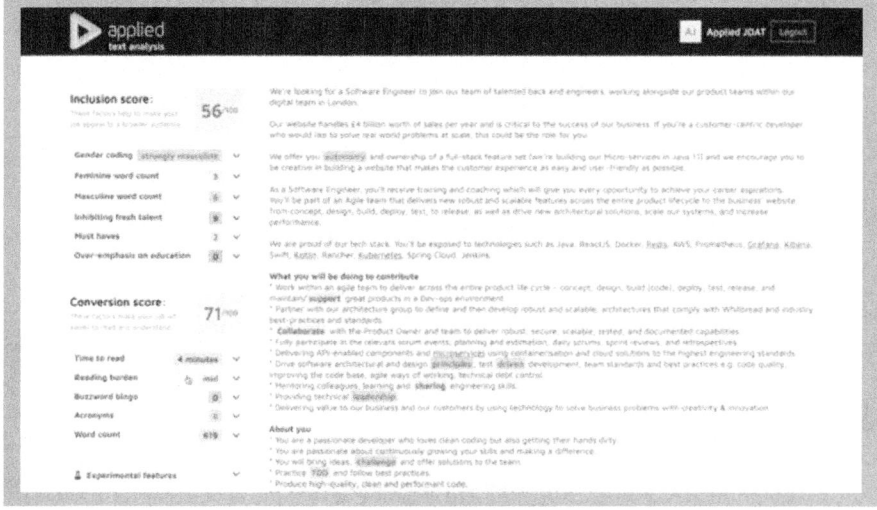

6. JobWriter.io

JobWriter happens to be a newer augmented writing tool to hit the market, but that doesn't make it any less effective than the others. In fact, JobWriter has a number of features that will help you write better job descriptions, including the ability to scan postings and highlight any words that you might consider changing in order to make the writing more gender-neutral.

It suggests alternatives for flagged words to make replacements quick and easy, too. However, you'll have to reach out to the company if you want information about pricing.

7. Joblint

Rating: Beginner

Features:

- Free tool that decodes your JD's
- Suggest alternative words to help attract diverse applicants

Allows you to test tech job posts for issues with sexism, culture, expectations, and recruiter fails. Keywords like Ninja, Go-Getter, or other terms can be a turn off to diverse candidates. This tools helps analyze your current openings and gives you suggestions on how to improve it.

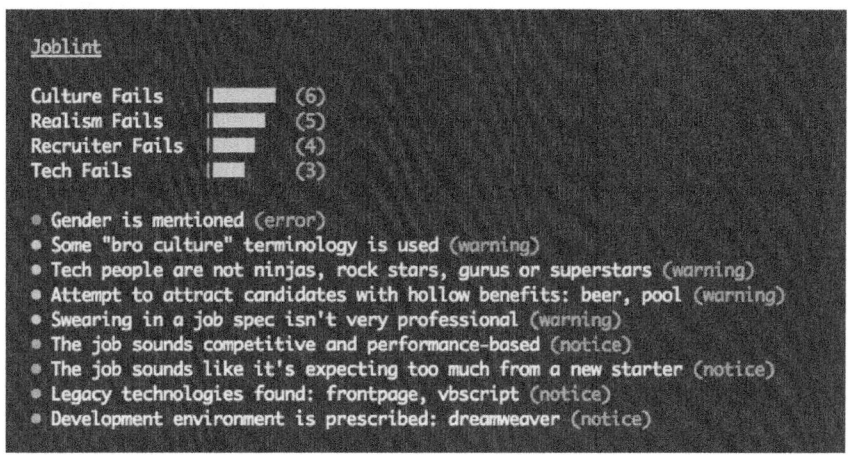

```
Joblint

Culture Fails    ▐███    (6)
Realism Fails    ▐██     (5)
Recruiter Fails  ▐███    (4)
Tech Fails       ▐██     (3)

● Gender is mentioned (error)
● Some "bro culture" terminology is used (warning)
● Tech people are not ninjas, rock stars, gurus or superstars (warning)
● Attempt to attract candidates with hollow benefits: beer, pool (warning)
● Swearing in a job spec isn't very professional (warning)
● The job sounds competitive and performance-based (notice)
● The job sounds like it's expecting too much from a new starter (notice)
● Legacy technologies found: frontpage, vbscript (notice)
● Development environment is prescribed: dreamweaver (notice)
```

8. Microsoft Word

Rating: Beginner

Features:

- Default tool within Microsoft word
- Free add-on that's simple and easy to use

Microsoft Word can help ensure inclusive language in professional communications by checking your writing for gender bias, age bias, and more. This feature is turned off by default, so if you want to avoid using exclusionary language, here's how to turn it on.

Start by opening a Microsoft Word document. From the "Home" tab, click Editor > Settings

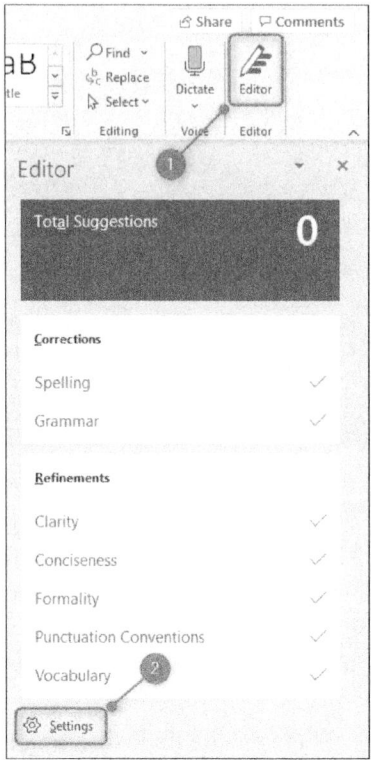

You can also access this menu by opening File > Options, choosing "Proofing," and then clicking the "Settings" button

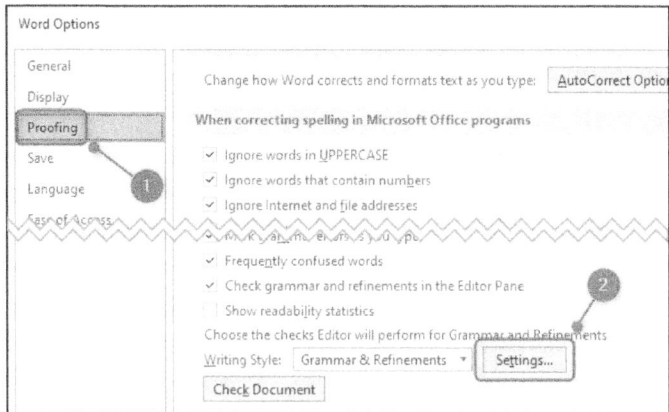

Scroll down to the "Inclusiveness" section, select all of the checkboxes that you want Word to check for in your documents, and click the "OK" button.

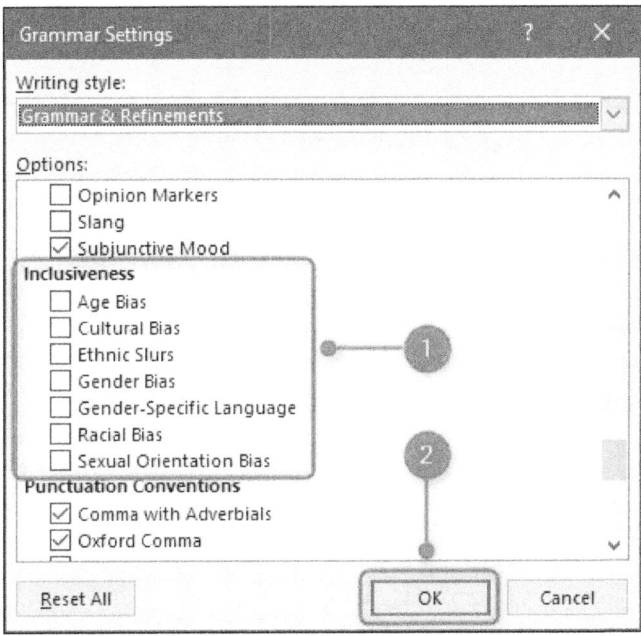

Now, when you write anything in Word, the grammar checker will pick up on non-inclusive languages, such as "whitelist" and "blacklist," and suggest alternatives.

Conclusion

I hope these Boolean string examples and talent sourcing tool suggestions will help you on your journey to find the best diverse talent for your opening. Talent sourcing takes a lot of effort and work, but it will pay off in the long run. Please check out my blog WizardSourcer.com for future updates.

Additional Resources:

Here's a list of over 200 Diversity terms that you can add into your search strings: https://blog.ongig.com/diversity-and-inclusion/diversity-terms/

I wanted to include a list of College, University, Alumni, Sororities, Fraternities, and Groups based in North America. Use this section to expand on your search.

Black Colleges and Universities in North America:
Alabama A&M University
Alabama State University
Albany State University
Alcorn State University
Allen University
American Baptist College
Arkansas Baptist College
Arkansas-Pine Bluff
Atlanta University Center
Barber-Scotia College
Benedict College
Bennett College
Bethune-Cookman University
Birmingham-Easonian Baptist Bible College
Bishop State Community College
Bluefield State College
Bowie State University
Carver College
Central State University
Charles Drew University of Medicine and Science
Cheyney University of Pennsylvania
Claflin University
Clark Atlanta University

Clinton College
Coahoma Community College
Concordia College
Coppin State University
Delaware State University
Denmark Technical College
Dillard University
Edward Waters College
Elizabeth City State University
Fayetteville State University
Fisk University
Florida A&M University
Florida Memorial University
Fort Valley State University
Gadsden State Community College
Grambling State University
H. Councill Trenholm State Community College
Hampton University
Harris-Stowe State University
Hinds Community College at Utica
Hood Theological
Howard University
Huston-Tillotson University
Interdenominational Theological Center
J. F. Drake State Technical College
Jackson State University
Jarvis Christian College
Johnson C Smith Theological Seminary
Johnson C. Smith University
Kentucky State University
Knoxville College
Lane College
Langston University
Lawson State Community College

LeMoyne-Owen College
Lewis College of Business
Lincoln University
Livingstone College
Meharry Medical College
Mid-Eastern Athletic Conference
Miles College
Miles School of Law
Mississippi Valley State University
Morehouse College
Morehouse School of Medicine
Morgan State University
Morris Brown College
Morris College
Norfolk State University
North Carolina A&T State University
North Carolina Central University
Oakwood University
Paine College
Paul Quinn College
Payne Theological
Philander Smith College
Prairie View A&M University
Rust College
Saint Paul's College
Savannah State University
Selma University
Shaw University
Shelton State Community College
Shorter College
Simmons College of Kentucky
South Carolina State University
Southern University and A&M College
Southern University at New Orleans

Southern University at Shreveport
Southwestern Athletic Conference
Southwestern Christian College
Spelman College
St. Augustine's University
St. Philip's College
Stillman College
Talladega College
Tennessee State University
Texas College
Texas Southern University
The Lincoln University
Tougaloo College
Tuskegee University
University of Arkansas at Pine Bluff
University of Maryland Eastern Shore
University of the District of Columbia
University of the Virgin Islands
Virginia State University
Virginia Union University
Virginia University of Lynchburg
Voorhees College
West Virginia State University
Wilberforce University
Wiley College
Winston-Salem State University
Xavier University of Louisiana

Top Black Fraternities and Sororities
Alpha Kappa Alpha
Alpha Kappa Nu
Alpha Phi Alpha
Beta Phi Pi
Delta Sigma Theta

Eta Phi Beta
Gamma Phi
Gamma Phi Delta
Gamma Tau
Groove Phi Groove
Improved Benevolent and Protective Order of Elks of the World
Iota Phi Lambda
Iota Phi Theta
Kappa Alpha Psi
Kappa Theta Epsilon
Malik Sigma Psi
Malika Kambe Umfazi
Megisté Areté
Nu Gamma Alpha
Omega Epsilon Rho Service Sorority
Omega Psi Phi
Phi Beta Sigma
Phi Delta Psi
Phi Rho Eta
Pi Gamma Omicron
Prince Hall Freemasonry
Sigma Gamma Rho
Sigma Phi Rho
Sigma Pi Phi
Swing Phi Swing
Tau Gamma Delta
Wine Psi Phi
Zeta Delta Phi
Zeta Phi Beta

Top Black Alumni Groups:
Africa Graduate Club of Notre Dame
African & Caribbean Villanovans
African American Alumni Association

African and Caribbean Students Association
African Cultural Studies Student Association
African Graduate Student Association
African Renaissance
African Society of Georgetown
African Student Organization
African Student Union
African Students Association
African-Carribean Culture Club
Africana Studies and Research Center
Africana Studies Club of Notre Dame
Afro-American Society at Dartmouth
Akanke
Association of Black Computer Scientists
Association of Black Students
Association of Rice University Black Alumni
Black Alumni Network of Tulane University
Black Alumni of MIT
Black Business Student Association
Black Caucus
Black Commerce Student Network
Black Community Services Center
Black Cultural Center
Black Cultural Society
Black Graduate and Professional Student Association
Black Graduate Caucus
Black Graduate Student Association
Black Graduate Student Organization
Black Graduation Committee
Black Honors Student Association
Black Jewish Alliance at UT Austin
Black Life Activism Club
Black Men Engaged
Black Muslims Alliance

Black Quare
Black Queer Collective
Black Resource Center
Black Senior Alliance
Black Student Assembly
Black Student Association of Notre Dame
Black Student Movement
Black Student Organization
Black Student Union
Black Students In Business
Black Students in Computer Science
Black Students' Union
Black Voices
Black Womyn's Collective
Blackwatch
Boston University Black Student Union
Brandeis African Students Organization
Brandeis Black Student Organization
Bruce D. Nesbitt African American Cultural Center
Caribbean Student Association
Caribbean Students Organization
Center for African Diaspora Student Success
Circle of Sisters
Divine Nine
Duke University Black Student Alliance
DukeAFRICA
Emory Black Student Union
Essence: Women of Color
Graduate Students of Color
Graduate Students of Color Collective
Haas Undergraduate Black Business Association
Haitian Student Unity
Hidden Dores
Hulon Willis Association

James Brister Society
National Council of Negro Women
National Society of Black Engineers
Northeastern African Student Organization
Northeastern Black Engineering Student Society
Northeastern Black Student Association
NYU Black Alumni Network
ONYX Magazine
Organization for African Students Interests and Solidarity
Penn African Students Association
Students of Color Alliance
Students of Color of Rackham
Tulane Black Student Union
USC Black Alumni Association
Voices: A Women of Color Collaborative
Wisconsin Association of Black Men
Wisconsin Black Student Union
Women of Color Alliance
Yale African American Affinity Group

Top Latinx Colleges and Universities in North America:
Adams State University
Aims Community College
Allan Hancock College
Altierus Career College-Thorton
Alvin Community College
Amarillo College
American River College
American University of Puerto Rico
Angelo State University
Antelope Valley College
Antillean Adventist University
Antioch University
Arizona State University

Arizona Western College
Atlantic University College
Austin Community College
Azusa Pacific University
Bakersfield College
Baptist University of the Americas
Barry University
Barstow Community College
Bayamon Central University
Bergen Community College
Berkeley City College
Big Bend Community College
Boricua College
Borough of Manhattan Community College
Brandman University
Brazosport College
Bronx Community College
Brookhaven College
Broward College
Butte College
Cabrillo College
California Baptist University
California Christian College
California College San Diego
California Lutheran University
California State Polytechnic University, Pomona
California State University, Bakersfield
California State University, Channel Islands
California State University, Chico
California State University, Dominguez Hills
California State University, East Bay
California State University, Fresno
California State University, Fullerton
California State University, Long Beach

California State University, Los Angeles
California State University, Monterey Bay
California State University, Northridge
California State University, Sacramento
California State University, San Bernardino
California State University, San Marcos
California State University, Stanislaus
Calumet College of Saint Joseph
Cañada College
Capital Community College
Caribbean University
Carlos Albizu University
Casa Loma College
CBD College
Central Arizona College
Central New Mexico Community College
Cerritos College
Cerro Coso Community College
Chabot College
Chaffey College
Chandler-Gilbert Community College
Charles R. Drew University of Medicine and Science
Cisco College
Citrus College
City College of New York
City College of San Francisco
City College-Miami
City Colleges of Chicago
Clovis Community College
Coastal Bend College
Coastline Community College
Cochise County Community College District
College of Alameda
College of Marin

College of Mount Saint Vincent
College of San Mateo
College of Southern Nevada
College of Staten Island
College of the Canyons
College of the Desert
College of the Sequoias
CollegeAmerica-Denver
CollegeAmerica-Fort Collins
CollegeAmerica-Phoenix
Colorado State University–Pueblo
Columbia Basin College
Community Christian College
Community College of Aurora
Community College of Denver
Compton College
Contra Costa College
Copper Mountain College
Cossatot Community College
Cosumnes River College
Crafton Hills College
Cuesta College
Cumberland County College
Cuyamaca College
Cypress College
Dalton State College
DeAnza College
Del Mar College
Diablo Valley College
Dodge City Community College
Dominican College
Dominican University
Doña Ana Community College
Donnelly College

East Los Angeles College
East San Gabriel Valley Regional Occupational Program
Eastern New Mexico University
Eastfield College
El Camino Community College District
El Centro College
El Paso Community College
Elgin Community College
Escuela de Artes Plásticas y Diseño de Puerto Rico
Essex County College
Estrella Mountain Community College
Evergreen Valley College
Fairleigh Dickinson University
Feather River Community College District
Felician University
First Nations University of Canada
Florida Atlantic University
Florida International University
Florida Keys Community College
Florida SouthWestern State College
Foothill College
Fresno City College
Fresno Pacific University
Fullerton College
Gabriel Dumont Institute
Galveston College
Gateway Community College
Gavilan College
Glendale Community College
Golden West College
Grossmont College
Guttman Community College
Hacienda La Puente Adult Education
Hallmark University

161

Hartnell College
Heritage University
Hillsborough Community College
Hodges University
Holy Names University
Hope International University
Housatonic Community College
Houston Baptist University
Houston Community College
Howard College
Hudson County Community College
Humboldt State University
Humphreys College
Hunter College
Imperial Valley College
Indian River State College
Jacksonville College
John Jay College of Criminal Justice
John Paul the Great Catholic University
Johnson & Wales University
Kean University
Keiser University
La Sierra University
Laguardia Community College
Lake Tahoe Community College
Lamar Community College
Laredo Community College
Las Positas College
Lassen Community College
Lee College
Lehman College
Life Pacific College
Loma Linda University
Lone Star College System

Long Beach City College
Los Angeles City College
Los Angeles County College of Nursing and Allied Health
Los Angeles Harbor College
Los Angeles Mission College
Los Angeles Pacific University
Los Angeles Pierce College
Los Angeles Southwest College
Los Angeles Trade–Technical College
Los Angeles Valley College
Los Medanos College
Marymount California University
McLennan Community College
Mendocino College
Menlo College
Merced College
Mercy College
Merritt College
Mesa Community College
Metropolitan State University of Denver
Miami Dade College
Middlebury Institute of International Studies at Monterey
Middlesex County College
Mills College
MiraCosta College
Mission College
Modesto Junior College
Monterey Peninsula College
Moorpark College
Moreno Valley College
Morgan Community College
Morton College
Mount Saint Mary's College
Mountain View College

Mt. San Antonio College
Mt. San Jacinto Community College District
Napa Valley College
National Louis University
National University
Naugatuck Valley Community College
New Jersey City University
New Mexico Highlands University
New Mexico Institute of Mining and Technology
New Mexico State University
New York City College of Technology
Norco College
North Lake College
Northeast Texas Community College
Northeastern Illinois University
Northern Essex Community College
Northern New Mexico College
Northwest Vista College
Northwood University
Norwalk Community College
Notre Dame de Namur University
Nova Southeastern University
Nyack College
Old Sun Community College
Orange Coast College
Orange County Community College
Otero Junior College
Our Lady of the Lake University
Oxnard College
Pacific Oaks College
Pacific Union College
Palm Beach State College
Palo Alto College
Palo Verde College

Palomar College
Pasadena City College
Passaic County Community College
Phoenix College
Pillar College
Pima Community College
Polytechnic University of Puerto Rico
Pontifical Catholic University of Puerto Rico
Porterville College
Providence Christian College
Pueblo Community College
Queens College
Reading Area Community College
Reedley College
Remington College
Rio Hondo College
Riverside City College
Robert Morris University Illinois
SABER College
Sacramento City College
Saddleback College
Saint John Vianney College Seminary
Saint Mary's College of California
Saint Peter's University
Saint Xavier University
San Antonio College
San Bernardino Valley College
San Diego Christian College
San Diego City College
San Diego Mesa College
San Diego Miramar College
San Diego State University
San Francisco State University
San Jacinto Community College

San Joaquin Delta College
San Jose City College
San Jose State University
San Juan Bautista School of Medicine
Santa Ana College
Santa Barbara City College
Santa Fe Community College
Santa Monica College
Santa Rosa Junior College
Santiago Canyon College
Schreiner University
Seminole State College of Florida
Seward County Community College
Sierra College
Six Nations Polytechnic
Skyline College
Solano Community College
Sonoma State University
South Florida State College
South Mountain Community College
South Plains College
South Texas College
Southern California University of Health Sciences
Southwest Texas Junior College
Southwestern Adventist University
Southwestern College
Springfield Technical Community College
St. Augustine College
St. Edward's University
St. Mary's University
St. Thomas University
Stevens Henager College
Sul Ross State University
Taft College

Tarrant County College
Texas A&M International University
Texas A&M University–Corpus Christi
Texas A&M University–Kingsville
Texas Lutheran University
Texas State University
Texas Tech University
Texas Woman's University
Trinidad State Junior College
Trinity International University-Florida
Trinity Washington University
Triton College
Union County College
Union Institute & University
Universidad del Este
Universidad del Sagrado Corazon
Universidad del Turabo
University of Arizona
University of Arizona South
University of California, Irvine
University of California, Merced
University of California, Riverside
University of California, Santa Barbara
University of California, Santa Cruz
University of Central Florida
University of Connecticut-Stamford
University of Houston
University of Illinois at Chicago
University of La Verne
University of New Mexico
University of North Carolina at Pembroke
University of Puerto Rico
University of Redlands
University of Saint Katherine

University of St. Thomas
University of Texas at Arlington
University of Texas at El Paso
University of Texas at San Antonio
University of Texas Health Science Center
University of Texas of the Permian Basin
University of Texas Rio Grande Valley
University of the Incarnate Word
University of the Southwest
University of the West
Urban College of Boston
Valencia College
Vanguard University of Southern California
Vaughn College of Aeronautics and Technology
Ventura College
Victor Valley College
Victoria College
Waubonsee Community College
Wenatchee Valley College
West Hills College Coalinga
West Hills College Lemoore
West Los Angeles College
West Valley College
Westchester Community College
Western New Mexico University
Western Texas College
Wharton County Junior College
Whittier College
Wilbur Wright College
William Paterson University
Woodbury University
Woodland Community College
Yakima Valley Community College
Yuba College

Top Latinx Fraternities and Sororities:
Alpha Pi Sigma
Alpha Psi Lambda
Alpha Rho Lambda
Alpha Theta Gamma
Beta Lambda Delta
Beta Xi Chi
Chi Upsilon Sigma
Delphic of Gamma Sigma Tau
Delta Alpha Omega
Delta Alpha Sigma
Delta Gamma Pi
Delta Psi Alpha
Delta Psi Sigma
Delta Sigma Chi
Delta Xi Nu
Delta Xi Phi
Epsilon Sigma Rho
Gamma Alpha Omega
Gamma Beta Lambda
Gamma Omega Delta
Gamma Phi Epsilon
Gamma Phi Omega
Gamma Zeta Alpha
Iota Nu Kappa
Kappa Delta Chi
Kappa Lambda Xi
Kappa Sigma Psi
Lambda Alpha Upsilon
Lambda Phi Xi
Lambda Pi Chi
Lambda Pi Upsilon
Lambda Psi Delta

Lambda Sigma Gamma
Lambda Sigma Upsilon
Lambda Tau Omega
Lambda Theta Alpha
Lambda Theta Nu
Lambda Theta Phi
Lambda Upsilon Lambda
Lambda Xi Beta
Mu Sigma Upsilon
Nu Alpha Kappa
Omega Delta
Omega Delta Phi
Omega Phi Beta
Omega Phi Chi
Omega Phi Kappa
Phi Chi Epsilon
Phi Iota Alpha
Psi Sigma Phi
Sigma Alpha Zeta
Sigma Beta Rho
Sigma Delta Alpha
Sigma Iota Alpha
Sigma Lambda Alpha
Sigma Lambda Beta
Sigma Lambda Gamma
Sigma Lambda Sigma
Sigma Lambda Upsilon
Sigma Omega Phi
Sigma Theta Psi
Tau Phi Sigma
Theta Delta Sigma
Theta Nu Kappa
Theta Nu Xi
Upsilon Kappa Delta

Zeta Chi Phi
Zeta Phi Rho
Zeta Sigma Chi

Top Indigenous Colleges and Universities in North America:
Aaniiih Nakoda College
Akitsiraq Law School
Anishinabek Education Institute
Bacone College
Bay Mills Community College
Blackfeet Community College
California Tribal College
Cankdeska Cikana Community College
Cheyenne and Arapaho Tribal College
Chief Dull Knife College
College of Menominee Nation
College of the Muscoggee Nation
Comanche Nation College
Diné College
First Nations Technical Institute, Tyendinaga Mohawk Territory
First Nations University of Canada
Fond du Lac Tribal and Community College
Fort Berthold Community College
Fort Peck Community College
Haskell Indian Nations University
Iḷisaġvik College
Institute of American Indian Arts
Iohahi:io Akwesasne Adult Education Centre
Kenjgewin Teg Educational Institute
Keweenaw Bay Ojibwa Community College
Lac Courte Oreilles Ojibwa Community College
Leech Lake Tribal College
Little Big Horn College
Little Priest Tribal College

Maskwachees Cultural College
Native Education Centre
Navajo Technical University
Nebraska Indian Community College
Negahneewin College
Nicola Valley Institute of Technology
Northwest Indian College
Nueta Hidatsa Sahnish College
Nunavut Arctic College
Oglala Lakota College
Ogwehoweh Skills and Trades Training Centre
Old Son Community College
Oshki-Pimache-O-Win Education & Training Institute
Pamulaan Center for Indigenous Peoples
Pawnee Nation College
Red Crow Community College
Red Lake Nation College
Saginaw Chippewa Tribal College
Salish Kootenai College
Salish Kootenai College
San Carlos Apache College
Saskatchewan Indian Institute of Technologies
Seven Generations Education Institute
Shingwauk Kinoomaage Gamig
Shingwauk Kinoomaage Gamig
Sinte Gleska University
Sisseton Wahpeton College
Sitting Bull College
Southwestern Indian Polytechnic Institute
Stone Child College
Tohono O'odham Community College
Turtle Mountain Community College
United Tribes Technical College
University College of the North

University nuhelot'įne thaiyots'į nistameyimâkanak Blue Quills
White Earth Tribal and Community College
Wind River Tribal College
Yellowhead Tribal College
Yellowquill College

Top Indigenous Fraternities and Sororities:
Alpha Pi Omega
Alpha Theta Gamma
Beta Lambda Delta
Beta Sigma Epsilon
Beta Xi Chi
Chi Sigma Xi
Delphic of Gamma Sigma Tau
Delta Alpha Omega
Delta Alpha Sigma
Delta Gamma Pi
Delta Psi Alpha
Delta Psi Sigma
Delta Xi Nu
Delta Xi Phi
Epsilon Chi Nu
Epsilon Sigma Rho
Gamma Beta Lambda
Gamma Delta Pi
Gamma Omega Delta
Gamma Phi Epsilon
Iota Nu Kappa
Kappa Lambda Xi
Kappa Sigma Psi
Lambda Phi Xi
Lambda Psi Delta
Lambda Sigma Gamma
Lambda Tau Omega

173

Lambda Xi Beta
Mu Sigma Upsilon
Omega Delta
Omega Delta Phi
Omega Phi Chi
Omega Phi Kappa
Phi Chi Epsilon
Phi Sigma Nu
Psi Sigma Phi
Sigma Alpha Zeta
Sigma Beta Rho
Sigma Lambda Gamma
Sigma Lambda Sigma
Sigma Nu Alpha Gamma
Sigma Omega Phi
Sigma Omicron Epsilon
Sigma Theta Psi
Tau Phi Sigma
Theta Delta Sigma
Theta Nu Kappa
Theta Nu Xi
Upsilon Kappa Delta
Zeta Chi Phi
Zeta Phi Rho
Zeta Sigma Chi

Boolean String Examples:

Black University Groups
("AHAA" OR "ALHF" OR "ALPFA" OR "ANPPM" OR
"CCNMA" OR "CHCI" OR "CHFC" OR "CHIRLA" OR
"CHLI" OR "CHSA" OR "Chicana" OR "Chicanas" OR
"Chicano" OR "Chicanos" OR "Culture Marketing Council" OR
"Dolores Huerta Foundation" OR "HACE" OR "HACR" OR

"HACU" OR "HNBA" OR "HSHPS" OR "Hermandad Mexicana Nacional" OR "Hispana" OR "Hispanic" OR "LATISM" OR "LCLAA" OR "LULAC" OR "La Raza Unida" OR "Latin America" OR "Latin American" OR "Latina" OR "Latina/o" OR "Latinas" OR "Latino" OR "Latinos" OR "League of United Latin American Citizens" OR "Mexican" OR "Mexican American" OR "NAHJ" OR "NALEO" OR "NCLR" OR "NHCC" OR "NHCOA" OR "NHMA" OR "National Association of Farmworker Organizations" OR "National Council of La Raza" OR "National Image, Inc" OR "New America Alliance" OR "NiLP" OR "Nosotros" OR "NosotrosPG" OR "Partido Nacional La Raza Unida" OR "Prospanica" OR "SHPE" OR "The LIBRE Initiative" OR "Tomas Rivera Policy Institute" OR "Tomás Rivera Policy Institute" OR "USHCC" OR "UnidosUS" OR "United Farm Workers of America" OR "VOCES Oral History" OR "Vida de Oro Foundation" OR "Voces Verdes" OR "del Barrio")

First Names in the US (Feminine)
("Abigail" OR "Adrienne" OR "Aimee" OR "Alexandra" OR "Alexis" OR "Alice" OR "Alicia" OR "Alisha" OR "Alison" OR "Allison" OR "Alyssa" OR "Amanda" OR "Amber" OR "Amy" OR "Ana" OR "Andrea" OR "Angel" OR "Angela" OR "Angelica" OR "Angie" OR "Anita" OR "Ann" OR "Anna" OR "Anne" OR "Annette" OR "Annie" OR "April" OR "Arlene" OR "Ashlee" OR "Ashley" OR "Audrey" OR "Autumn" OR "Barbara" OR "Becky" OR "Belinda" OR "Beth" OR "Bethany" OR "Betty" OR "Beverly" OR "Bonnie" OR "Brandi" OR "Brandy" OR "Brenda" OR "Brianna" OR "Bridget" OR "Brittany" OR "Brittney" OR "Brooke" OR "Caitlin" OR "Candace" OR "Candice" OR "Carla" OR "Carmen" OR "Carol" OR "Carole" OR "Caroline" OR "Carolyn" OR "Carrie" OR "Casey" OR "Cassandra" OR "Cassie" OR "Catherine" OR "Cathy" OR "Charlene" OR "Charlotte" OR "Chelsea" OR

"Cheryl" OR "Christie" OR "Christina" OR "Christine" OR "Christy" OR "Cindy" OR "Claudia" OR "Colleen" OR "Connie" OR "Constance" OR "Courtney" OR "Cristina" OR "Crystal" OR "Cynthia" OR "Dana" OR "Danielle" OR "Darlene" OR "Dawn" OR "Deanna" OR "Debbie" OR "Deborah" OR "Debra" OR "Delores" OR "Denise" OR "Desiree" OR "Diana" OR "Diane" OR "Dianne" OR "Dolores" OR "Dominique" OR "Donna" OR "Doreen" OR "Doris" OR "Dorothy" OR "Ebony" OR "Eileen" OR "Elaine" OR "Elizabeth" OR "Ellen" OR "Emily" OR "Erica" OR "Erika" OR "Erin" OR "Eva" OR "Evelyn" OR "Felicia" OR "Frances" OR "Gail" OR "Gayle" OR "Geraldine" OR "Gina" OR "Glenda" OR "Gloria" OR "Grace" OR "Gwendolyn" OR "Hannah" OR "Heather" OR "Heidi" OR "Helen" OR "Holly" OR "Irene" OR "Jackie" OR "Jaclyn" OR "Jacqueline" OR "Jaime" OR "Jamie" OR "Jan" OR "Jane" OR "Janet" OR "Janice" OR "Janis" OR "Jasmine" OR "Jean" OR "Jeanette" OR "Jeanne" OR "Jenna" OR "Jennifer" OR "Jenny" OR "Jessica" OR "Jill" OR "Jillian" OR "Jo" OR "Joan" OR "Joann" OR "Joanna" OR "Joanne" OR "Jodi" OR "Jody" OR "Jordan" OR "Josephine" OR "Joy" OR "Joyce" OR "Juanita" OR "Judith" OR "Judy" OR "Julia" OR "Julie" OR "June" OR "Kara" OR "Karen" OR "Kari" OR "Karla" OR "Katelyn" OR "Katherine" OR "Kathleen" OR "Kathryn" OR "Kathy" OR "Katie" OR "Katrina" OR "Kay" OR "Kayla" OR "Kelli" OR "Kellie" OR "Kelly" OR "Kelsey" OR "Kendra" OR "Kerri" OR "Kerry" OR "Kim" OR "Kimberly" OR "Krista" OR "Kristen" OR "Kristi" OR "Kristie" OR "Kristin" OR "Kristina" OR "Kristine" OR "Kristy" OR "Krystal" OR "Lacey" OR "Latasha" OR "Latoya" OR "Laura" OR "Lauren" OR "Laurie" OR "Leah" OR "Leslie" OR "Lillian" OR "Linda" OR "Lindsay" OR "Lindsey" OR "Lisa" OR "Lois" OR "Loretta" OR "Lori" OR "Lorraine" OR "Louise" OR "Lynda" OR "Lynn" OR "Lynne" OR "Mallory" OR "Mandy" OR "Marcia" OR "Margaret" OR "Maria" OR "Marianne" OR "Marie" OR "Marilyn" OR

"Marissa" OR "Marjorie" OR "Marlene" OR "Marsha" OR "Martha" OR "Mary" OR "Maureen" OR "Meagan" OR "Megan" OR "Meghan" OR "Melanie" OR "Melinda" OR "Melissa" OR "Melody" OR "Meredith" OR "Michele" OR "Michelle" OR "Mildred" OR "Mindy" OR "Miranda" OR "Misty" OR "Molly" OR "Monica" OR "Monique" OR "Morgan" OR "Nancy" OR "Natalie" OR "Natasha" OR "Nichole" OR "Nicole" OR "Nina" OR "Norma" OR "Olivia" OR "Pam" OR "Pamela" OR "Patricia" OR "Patsy" OR "Patti" OR "Patty" OR "Paula" OR "Peggy" OR "Penny" OR "Phyllis" OR "Priscilla" OR "Rachael" OR "Rachel" OR "Rebecca" OR "Rebekah" OR "Regina" OR "Renee" OR "Rhonda" OR "Rita" OR "Roberta" OR "Robin" OR "Robyn" OR "Rosa" OR "Rose" OR "Rosemary" OR "Roxanne" OR "Ruby" OR "Ruth" OR "Sabrina" OR "Sally" OR "Samantha" OR "Sandra" OR "Sandy" OR "Sara" OR "Sarah" OR "Shannon" OR "Shari" OR "Sharon" OR "Shawna" OR "Sheena" OR "Sheila" OR "Shelia" OR "Shelley" OR "Shelly" OR "Sheri" OR "Sherri" OR "Sherry" OR "Sheryl" OR "Shirley" OR "Sonia" OR "Sonya" OR "Stacey" OR "Stacie" OR "Stacy" OR "Stefanie" OR "Stephanie" OR "Sue" OR "Susan" OR "Suzanne" OR "Sylvia" OR "Tabitha" OR "Tamara" OR "Tami" OR "Tammie" OR "Tammy" OR "Tanya" OR "Tara" OR "Tasha" OR "Taylor" OR "Teresa" OR "Terri" OR "Terry" OR "Theresa" OR "Tiffany" OR "Tina" OR "Toni" OR "Tonya" OR "Tracey" OR "Traci" OR "Tracie" OR "Tracy" OR "Tricia" OR "Valerie" OR "Vanessa" OR "Veronica" OR "Vicki" OR "Vickie" OR "Vicky" OR "Victoria" OR "Virginia" OR "Vivian" OR "Wanda" OR "Wendy" OR "Whitney" OR "Yolanda" OR "Yvette" OR "Yvonne")

Spanish First Names (Feminine)
("Adan" OR "Alberto" OR "Alejandro" OR "Alfonso" OR "Alfredo" OR "Alonso" OR "Alonzo" OR "Alvaro" OR "Antonio" OR "Arlo" OR "Armando" OR "Benicio" OR

"Carlos" OR "Carmelo" OR "Cesar" OR "Cristian" OR
"Cristiano" OR "Cruz" OR "Diego" OR "Eduardo" OR
"Emiliano" OR "Emilio" OR "Enrique" OR "Ernesto" OR
"Esteban" OR "Ezequiel" OR "Felipe" OR "Fernando" OR
"Francisco" OR "Gerardo" OR "Guillermo" OR "Gustavo" OR
"Hugo" OR "Ignacio" OR "Isaias" OR "Ismael" OR "Jadiel" OR
"Jaime" OR "Javier" OR "Joaquin" OR "Jorge" OR "Jose" OR
"Juan" OR "Julio" OR "Leandro" OR "Leonardo" OR "Leonel"
OR "Lorenzo" OR "Luciano" OR "Manuel" OR "Marcelo" OR
"Marco" OR "Marcos" OR "Mario" OR "Mateo" OR "Matias"
OR "Mauricio" OR "Maximiliano" OR "Maximo" OR "Miguel"
OR "Moises" OR "Pablo" OR "Pedro" OR "Rafael" OR "Raul"
OR "Rey" OR "Ricardo" OR "Roberto" OR "Rodrigo" OR
"Rogelio" OR "Salvador" OR "Santana" OR "Santiago" OR
"Sergio" OR "Tadeo" OR "Ulises" OR "Valentino" OR
"Vicente")

Latin Organizations
("AHAA" OR "ALHF" OR "ALPFA" OR "ANPPM" OR
"CCNMA" OR "CHCI" OR "CHFC" OR "CHIRLA" OR
"CHLI" OR "CHSA" OR "Chicana" OR "Chicanas" OR
"Chicano" OR "Chicanos" OR "Culture Marketing Council" OR
"Dolores Huerta Foundation" OR "HACE" OR "HACR" OR
"HACU" OR "HNBA" OR "HSHPS" OR "Hermandad Mexicana
Nacional" OR "Hispana" OR "Hispanic" OR "LATISM" OR
"LCLAA" OR "LULAC" OR "La Raza Unida" OR "Latin
America" OR "Latin American" OR "Latina" OR "Latina/o" OR
"Latinas" OR "Latino" OR "Latinos" OR "League of United
Latin American Citizens" OR "Mexican" OR "Mexican
American" OR "NAHJ" OR "NALEO" OR "NCLR" OR
"NHCC" OR "NHCOA" OR "NHMA" OR "National
Association of Farmworker Organizations" OR "National
Council of La Raza" OR "National Image, Inc" OR "New
America Alliance" OR "NiLP" OR "Nosotros" OR

"NosotrosPG" OR "Partido Nacional La Raza Unida" OR "Prospanica" OR "SHPE" OR "The LIBRE Initiative" OR "Tomas Rivera Policy Institute" OR "Tomás Rivera Policy Institute" OR "USHCC" OR "UnidosUS" OR "United Farm Workers of America" OR "VOCES Oral History" OR "Vida de Oro Foundation" OR "Voces Verdes" OR "del Barrio")

Diverse LGBT Organizations
("Adodi" OR "At the Beach LA" OR "Ball culture" OR "Black AIDS Institute" OR "D.C. Black Pride" OR "Dallas Black Pride" OR "Flava Works" OR "Hotter than July" OR "LGBT Detroit" OR "National Black Justice Coalition" OR "Salsa Soul Sisters" OR "The Okra Project" OR "The Portal (community center)"

Diverse LinkedIn Groups
("accountant of color" OR "accountants of color" OR "african accountant" OR "african accountants" OR "african achievement" OR "african affinity" OR "african alliance" OR "african alumni" OR "african america" OR "african american" OR "african americans" OR "african business" OR "african businesses" OR "african career" R "african careers" OR "african chamber of commerce" OR "african chambers" OR "african child" OR "african children" OR "african communities" OR "african community" OR "african designers" OR "african economic" OR "african employee" OR "african employees" OR "african engineer" OR "african engineers" OR "african enterprise" OR "african enterprises" OR "african erg" OR "african excellence" OR "african executive" OR "african executives" OR "african female" OR "african girl" OR "african girls" OR "african health" OR "african heritage" OR "african hotel" OR "african justice" OR "african law students" OR "african leaders" OR "african leadership" OR "african male" OR "african man" OR "african mba" OR "african men" OR "african men's" OR "african nurses" OR "african organizers" OR "african owned" OR "african

people" OR "african physicists" OR "african pride" OR "african professional" OR "african professionals" OR "african resource" OR "african society" OR "african software engineers" OR "african storytellers" OR "african student" OR "african students" OR "african usa" OR "african wall street" OR "african woman" OR "african women" OR "african women's" OR "african youth" OR "alumni of color" OR "americans of color" OR "black accountant" OR "black accountants" OR "black achievement" OR "black affinity" OR "black alliance" OR "black alumni" OR "black america" OR "black american" OR "black americans" OR "black business" OR "black businesses" OR "black career" OR "black careers" OR "black chamber of commerce" OR "black chambers" OR "black child" OR "black children" OR "black communities" OR "black community" OR "black designers" OR "black economic" OR "black employee" OR "black employees" OR "black engineer" OR "black engineers" OR "black enterprise" OR "black enterprises" OR "black erg" OR "black excellence" OR "black executive" OR "black executives" OR "black female" OR "black girl" OR "black girls" OR "black googler" OR "black health" OR "black heritage" OR "black hotel" OR "black justice" OR "black law students" OR "black leaders" OR "black leadership" OR "black male" OR "black man" OR "black mba" OR "black men" OR "black men's" OR "black nurses" OR "black organizers" OR "black owned" OR "black people" OR "black physicists" OR "black power" OR "black pride" OR "black professional" OR "black professionals" OR "black resource" OR "black society" OR "black software engineers" OR "black storytellers" OR "black student" OR "black students" OR "black usa" OR "black wall street" OR "black woman" OR "black women" OR "black women's" OR "black youth" OR "business of color" OR "businesses of color" OR "careers of color" OR "child of color" OR "children of color" OR "communities of color" OR "community of color" OR "designers of color" OR "employee of color" OR "employees of color" OR "engineer of color" OR "engineers of color" OR "enterprise of color" OR "enterprises of color" OR "executive of color" OR "executives of color" OR "girls of color" OR "law students of color" OR "leaders of color" OR "man of color" OR "mba of color" OR "men of color" OR "nurses of color" OR "organizers of color" OR "people of color" OR "physicists of color" OR "professional of color" OR "professionals of color" OR "society of color" OR "software engineers of color" OR "storytellers of color" OR "student of color" OR "students of color" OR "woman of color" OR "women of color" OR "youth of color")

Women's Rights Organizations
("AHA Foundation" OR "African Queens and Women Cultural Leaders Network" OR "African Women on Board" OR "Agape International Missions" OR "Ain o Salish Kendra" OR "All India Democratic n's Association" OR "All Women's Action Society" OR "All-Poland Women's Strike" OR "Alpha Kappa Alpha" OR "Arab Feminist Union" OR "Asociación Nacional de Mujeres Españolas" OR "Asociación para la Enseñanza de la Mujer" OR "Association internationale des femmes" OR "Association pour le Droit des Femmes" OR "Associazione per la donna" OR "Asuda" OR "Atene Femenino" OR "BRAC" OR "Bangladesh Mahila Parishad" OR "Bangladesh Mahila Samiti" OR "Blackburn Female Reform Society" OR "Bonhishikha" OR "Canadian Unitarian Universalist Women's Association" OR "Capazes" OR "Centrum Praw Kobiet" OR "Chanyang-hoe" OR "Chicana Rights Project" OR "Chifuren" OR "Comitato pro suffragio femminile" OR "Connecticut Woman Suffrage Association" OR "Consiglio Nazionale delle Donne Italiane" OR "Danish Women's Society" OR "Danske Kvindeforenings Valgsretsudvalg" OR "Delta Sigma Theta" OR "DeltaWomen" OR "Durbar Mahila Samanwaya Committee" OR "European Women's Lobby" OR "Fawcett Society" OR "FreeThe20

campaign" OR "Freedom (charity)" OR "Fusen Kakutoku Dōmei" OR "Gender Equality Architecture Reform" OR "Gender Studies and Human Rights Documentation Centre" OR "Girls Not Brides" OR "Instituto Promundo" OR "International Women's Development Agency" OR "Ipas" OR "Islands Society" OR "Jesuit Volunteer Corps" OR "Kappa Theta Epsilon" OR "Kensington Society" OR "Korea Women's Hot Line" OR "Kurdish Women's Rights Watch" OR "Landesa" OR "Lega promotrice degli interessi femminili" OR "Les amis du bus des femmes" OR "Liga Drepturilor şi Datoriilor Femeilor" OR "Liga Femeilor Române" OR "Ligue Française pour le Droit des Femmes" OR "MATCH International Women's Fund" OR "Mama Cash" OR "Mona Foundation" OR "Mujer y Salud en Uruguay" OR "Myanmar Women's Affairs Federation" OR "Naisasialiitto Unioni" OR "Narika" OR "National Advisory Council on Violence Against Women" OR "National Equal Rights Party" OR "National Network to End Domestic Violence" OR "New Japan Women's League" OR "New Women's Association" OR "New York Asian Women's Centre" OR "New York City Council Women's Caucus" OR "Nigerian Women's Trust Fund" OR "Norwegian Women's Lobby" OR "Nüzi canzheng tongmenghui" OR "POWA" OR "Prince Edward Island Reproductive Rights Organization" OR "Prizm Project" OR "Rasan" OR "Reaching Out Romania" OR "Renew Foundation" OR "Sigma Gamma Rho" OR "Sigma Lambda Gamma" OR "Sisterhood Is Global Institute" OR "Societatea Ortodoxă Naţională a Femeilor Române" OR "Splošno slovensko žensko društvo" OR "Sunseong-hoe" OR "Survivors Foundation" OR "Tanzania Media Women's Association" OR "Tartu Eesti Naesterahva Selts" OR "Tesselschade-Arbeid Adelt" OR "Texas Equal Rights Association" OR "The Five Foundation" OR "The Third Billion" OR "The White House Project" OR "The Womanity Foundation" OR "The Women's Conference" OR "Theta Nu Xi" OR "Third World Women's

Alliance" OR "Tokyo Rengo Fujinkai" OR "UN Women" OR "UltraViolet" OR "Union des femmes de Wallonie" OR "UniteWomen.org" OR "Unión de Mujeres Americanas" OR "Vereeniging voor Vrouwenkiesrecht" OR "Vital Voices" OR "Vrije Vrouwen Vereeniging" OR "White Hands Campaign" OR "WomanStats Project" OR "Women Under Siege Project" OR "Women and Memory Forum" OR "Women's International Zionist Organization" OR "Women's Voices Now" OR "Women's Way" OR "Yugoslav Women's Alliance")

Black Tech Groups
("AAUW" OR "ACM W" OR "Illinois connections in engineering" OR "MEP" OR "NSBE" OR "National society of black enginees" OR "adcolor industry coalition" OR "allstarcode" OR "blacks in tech" OR "blacks in technology" OR "gates millennium scholars program" OR "generation google scholarships" OR "hack the hood" OR "hidden genius project" OR "minority alliance in computer science" OR "morrill engineering program" OR "national action council for minorities in engineering" OR "society of black scientists and engineers" OR "united negro college fund" OR "year up")

Latin Tech Groups
("AAUW" OR "ACM W" OR "MEP" OR "NACME" OR "NAMEPA" OR "National Action Council for Minorities in Engineering" OR "National Association of Multicultural Engineering Program Advocates" OR "Society of Hispanic Professional Engineers Foundation" OR "illinois connections in engineering" OR "latina computer science club" OR "latinas in computer science" OR "latino computer science club" OR "latino/a computer science club" OR "latinos in computer science" OR "lcsc google coding competition" OR "minority alliance in computer science" OR "morrill engineering program" OR "national action council for minorities in engineering")

Women Tech Groups

("AAUW" OR "ACM W" OR "Alliance of Technology and
Women" OR "America's Women's Community" OR "American
Association of University Women" OR "Association for Women
in Computing" OR "Girl Scouts of America" OR "GirlGeeks"
OR "Grace Hopper" OR "HighTech Women" OR "MEP" OR "Pi
Beta Phi" OR "Society of Women in GIS" OR "TechDivas" OR
"anitaborg" OR "association for women in computing" OR
"illinois connections in engineering" OR "minority alliance in
computer science" OR "morrill engineering program" OR
"national action council for minorities in engineering" OR
"society of women SWE" OR "society of women engineers" OR
"webgrrls" OR "wics" OR "women active in computer science"
OR "women in computer science" OR "women in engineering")

Sources:

1. *Qcc.cuny.edu – Diversity Defined*
2. *Diversifytech.co - Diversity Definitions*
3. *Glassdoor.com – Hiring Data*
4. *Wikipedia.com – Demographic Data*
5. *NativeCurrent.com – Boolean string examples*

Printed in Great Britain
by Amazon